NON SANZ DROICT.

William Shakespeare

A MIDSUMMER NIGHT'S DREAM

Edited by Wolfgang Clemen

The Signet Classic Shakespeare
GENERAL EDITOR: SYLVAN BARNET

A SIGNET CLASSIC
PUBLISHED BY THE NEW AMERICAN LIBRARY, NEW YORK
AND TORONTO
THE NEW ENGLISH LIBRARY LIMITED, LONDON

Fourth Printing

SIGNET TRADEMARK REG. U.S. PAT. OFF. AND FOREIGN COUNTRIES
REGISTERED TRADEMARK—MARCA REGISTRADA
HECHO EN CHICAGO, U.S.A.

SIGNET CLASSICS are published *in the United States* by
The New American Library, Inc.,
1301 Avenue of the Americas, New York, New York 10019,
in Canada by The New American Library of Canada Limited,
295 King Street East, Toronto 2, Ontario,
in the United Kingdom by The New English Library Limited,
Barnard's Inn, Holborn, London, E.C. 1, England

PRINTED IN THE UNITED STATES OF AMERICA

Contents

Shakespeare: Prefatory Remarks

Between the record of his baptism in Stratford on 26 April 1564 and the record of his burial in Stratford on 25 April 1616, some forty documents name Shakespeare, and many others name his parents, his children, and his grandchildren. More facts are known about William Shakespeare than about any other playwright of the period except Ben Jonson. The facts should, however, be distinguished from the legends. The latter, inevitably more engaging and better known, tell us that the Stratford boy killed a calf in high style, poached deer and rabbits, and was forced to flee to London, where he held horses outside a playhouse. These traditions are only traditions; they may be true, but no evidence supports them, and it is well to stick to the facts.

Mary Arden, the dramatist's mother, was the daughter of a substantial landowner; about 1557 she married John Shakespeare, who was a glove-maker and trader in various farm commodities. In 1557 John Shakespeare was a member of the Council (the governing body of Stratford), in 1558 a constable of the borough, in 1561 one of the two town chamberlains, in 1565 an alderman (entitling him to the appellation "Mr."), in 1568 high bailiff—the town's highest political office, equivalent to mayor. After 1577, for an unknown reason he drops out of local politics. The birthday of William Shakespeare, the eldest son of this locally prominent man, is unrecorded; but the Stratford parish register records that the infant was baptized on 26 April 1564. (It is quite possible that he was born on 23 April, but this date has probably been assigned by tradition because it is the date on which, fifty-two years later, he died.) The attendance records of the Stratford grammar school of the period are not extant, but it is reasonable to assume that the son of a local official attended the school and received substantial training in Latin. The masters of the school from Shakespeare's seventh to fifteenth years held Oxford degrees; the Elizabethan curriculum excluded mathematics and the natural sciences but taught a good deal of Latin rhetoric, logic, and literature. On 27 November 1582 a marriage license was issued to Shakespeare and Anne Hathaway, eight years his senior. The couple had a child in May, 1583. Perhaps the marriage was necessary, but perhaps the couple had earlier engaged in a formal "troth plight" which would render their children legitimate even if no further ceremony were performed. In 1585 Anne Hathaway bore Shakespeare twins.

That Shakespeare was born is excellent; that he married and had children is pleasant; but that we know nothing about his departure from Stratford to London, or about the beginning of his theatrical career, is lamentable and must be admitted. We would gladly sacrifice details about his children's baptism for details about his earliest days on the stage. Perhaps the poaching episode is true (but it is first reported almost a century after Shakespeare's death), or perhaps he first left Stratford to be a schoolteacher, as another tradition holds; perhaps he was moved by

> Such wind as scatters young men through the world,
> To seek their fortunes further than at home
> Where small experience grows.

In 1592, thanks to the cantankerousness of Robert Greene, a rival playwright and a pamphleteer, we have our first reference, a snarling one, to Shakespeare as an actor and playwright. Greene warns those of his own educated friends who wrote for the theater against an actor who has presumed to turn playwright:

There is an upstart crow, beautified with our feathers,
that with his *tiger's heart wrapped in a player's hide* supposes he is as well able to bombast out a blank verse as
the best of you, and being an absolute Johannes-factotum
is in his own conceit the only Shake-scene in a country.

The reference to the player, as well as the allusion to
Aesop's crow (who strutted in borrowed plumage, as an
actor struts in fine words not his own), makes it clear
that by this date Shakespeare had both acted and written.
That Shakespeare is meant is indicated not only by
"Shake-scene" but by the parody of a line from one of
Shakespeare's plays, *3 Henry VI:* "O, tiger's heart
wrapped in a woman's hide." If Shakespeare in 1592 was
prominent enough to be attacked by an envious dramatist,
he probably had served an apprenticeship in the theater
for at least a few years.

In any case, by 1592 Shakespeare had acted and
written, and there are a number of subsequent references
to him as an actor: documents indicate that in 1598 he is
a "principal comedian," in 1603 a "principal tragedian,"
in 1608 he is one of the "men players." The profession
of actor was not for a gentleman, and it occasionally
drew the scorn of university men who resented writing
speeches for persons less educated than themselves, but
it was respectable enough: players, if prosperous, were in
effect members of the bourgeoisie, and there is nothing
to suggest that Stratford considered William Shakespeare
less than a solid citizen. When, in 1596, the Shakespeares
were granted a coat of arms, the grant was made to
Shakespeare's father, but probably William Shakespeare
(who the next year bought the second-largest house in
town) had arranged the matter on his own behalf. In
subsequent transactions he is occasionally styled a gentleman.

Although in 1593 and 1594 Shakespeare published two
narrative poems dedicated to the Earl of Southampton,
Venus and Adonis and *The Rape of Lucrece,* and may
well have written most or all of his sonnets in the middle nineties, Shakespeare's literary activity seems to have

been almost entirely devoted to the theater. (It may be significant that the two narrative poems were written in years when the plague closed the theaters for several months.) In 1594 he was a charter member of a theatrical company called the Chamberlain's Men (which in 1603 changed its name to the King's Men); until he retired to Stratford (about 1611, apparently), he was with this remarkably stable company. From 1599 the company acted primarily at the Globe Theatre, in which Shakespeare held a one-tenth interest. Other Elizabethan dramatists are known to have acted, but no other is known also to have been entitled to a share in the profits of the playhouse.

Shakespeare's first eight published plays did not have his name on them, but this is not remarkable; the most popular play of the sixteenth century, Thomas Kyd's *The Spanish Tragedy,* went through many editions without naming Kyd, and Kyd's authorship is known only because a book on the profession of acting happens to quote (and attribute to Kyd) some lines on the interest of Roman emperors in the drama. What is remarkable is that after 1598 Shakespeare's name commonly appears on printed plays—some of which are not his. Another indication of his popularity comes from Francis Meres, author of *Palladis Tamia: Wit's Treasury* (1598): in this anthology of snippets accompanied by an essay on literature, many playwrights are mentioned, but Shakespeare's name occurs more often than any other, and Shakespeare is the only playwright whose plays are listed.

From his acting, playwriting, and share in a theater, Shakespeare seems to have made considerable money. He put it to work, making substantial investments in Stratford real estate. When he made his will (less than a month before he died), he sought to leave his property intact to his descendants. Of small bequests to relatives and to friends (including three actors, Richard Burbage, John Heminges, and Henry Condell), that to his wife of the second-best bed has provoked the most comment; perhaps it was the bed the couple had slept in, the best being reserved for visitors. In any case, had Shakespeare not excepted it, the bed would have gone (with the rest of his household possessions) to his daughter and her husband. On 25 April 1616 he was buried within the chancel of the church at Stratford. An unattractive monument to his memory, placed on a wall near the grave, says he died on 23 April. Over the grave itself are the lines, perhaps by Shakespeare, that (more than his literary fame) have kept his bones undisturbed in the crowded burial ground where old bones were often dislodged to make way for new:

> Good friend, for Jesus' sake forbear
> To dig the dust enclosèd here.
> Blessed be the man that spares these stones
> And cursed be he that moves my bones.

Thirty-seven plays, as well as some nondramatic poems, are held to constitute the Shakespeare canon. The dates of composition of most of the works are highly uncertain, but there is often evidence of a *terminus a quo* (starting point) and/or a *terminus ad quem* (terminal point) that provides a framework for intelligent guessing. For example, *Richard II* cannot be earlier than 1595, the publication date of some material to which it is indebted; *The Merchant of Venice* cannot be later than 1598, the year Francis Meres mentioned it. Sometimes arguments for a date hang on an alleged topical allusion, such as the lines about the unseasonable weather in *A Midsummer Night's Dream,* II.i.81–87, but such an allusion (if indeed it is an allusion) can be variously interpreted, and in any case there is always the possibility that a topical allusion was inserted during a revision, years after the composition of a play. Dates are often attributed on the basis of style, and although conjectures about style usually rest on other conjectures, sooner or later one must rely on one's literary sense. There is no real proof, for example, that *Othello* is not as early as *Romeo and Juliet,* but one feels *Othello* is later, and because the first record of its performance is 1604, one is glad enough to set its composition at that date and not push it back into Shakespeare's early years. The following chronology, then, is as much indebted to informed guesswork and sensitivity as it is to fact. The dates, necessarily imprecise, indicate something like a scholarly consensus.

PLAYS

Shakespeare's Theater

In Shakespeare's infancy, Elizabethan actors performed wherever they could—in great halls, at court, in the court-yards of inns. The innyards must have made rather un-satisfactory theaters: on some days they were unavailable because carters bringing goods to London used them as depots; when available, they had to be rented from the innkeeper; perhaps most important, London inns were subject to the Common Council of London, which was not well disposed toward theatricals. In 1574 the Common Council required that plays and playing places in London be licensed. It asserted that

> sundry great disorders and inconveniences have been found to ensue to this city by the inordinate haunting of great multitudes of people, specially youth, to plays, inter-ludes, and shows, namely occasion of frays and quarrels, evil practices of incontinency in great inns having cham-bers and secret places adjoining to their open stages and galleries,

and ordered that innkeepers who wished licenses to hold performances put up a bond and make contributions to the poor.

The requirement that plays and innyard theaters be licensed, along with the other drawbacks of playing at inns, probably drove James Burbage (a carpenter-turned-actor) to rent in 1576 a plot of land northeast of the city walls and to build here—on property outside the jurisdiction of the city—England's first permanent construction designed for plays. He called it simply the Theatre. About all that is known of its construction is that it was wood. It soon had imitators, the most famous being the Globe (1599), built across the Thames (again outside the city's jurisdiction), out of timbers of the Theatre, which had been dismantled when Burbage's lease ran out.

There are three important sources of information about the structure of Elizabethan playhouses—drawings, a contract, and stage directions in plays. Of drawings, only the so-called De Witt drawing (c. 1596) of the Swan—really a friend's copy of De Witt's drawing—is of much significance. It shows a building of three tiers, with a stage jutting from a wall into the yard or center of the building. The tiers are roofed, and part of the stage is covered by a roof that projects from the rear and is supported at its front on two posts, but the groundlings, who paid a penny to stand in front of the stage, were exposed to the sky. (Performances in such a playhouse were held only in the daytime; artificial illumination was not used.) At the rear of the stage are two doors; above the stage is a gallery. The second major source of information, the contract for the Fortune, specifies that although the Globe is to be the model, the Fortune is to be square, eighty feet outside and fifty-five inside. The stage is to be forty-three feet broad, and is to extend into the middle of the yard (i.e., it is twenty-seven and a half feet deep). For patrons willing to pay more than the general admission charged of the groundlings, there were to be three galleries provided with seats. From the third chief source, stage directions, one learns that entrance to the stage was by doors, presumably spaced widely apart at the rear ("Enter one citizen at one door, and another at the other"), and that in addition to the platform stage there was occasionally some sort of curtained booth or alcove allowing for "discovery" scenes, and some sort of playing space "aloft" or "above" to represent (for example) the top of a city's walls or a room above the street. Doubtless each theater had its own peculiarities, but perhaps we can talk about a "typical" Elizabethan theater if we realize that no theater need exactly have fit the description, just as no father is the typical father with 3.7 children. This hypothetical theater is wooden, round or polygonal (in *Henry V* Shakespeare calls it a "wooden *O*"), capable of holding some eight hundred spectators standing in the yard around the projecting elevated stage and some fifteen hundred additional spectators seated in the three roofed galleries. The stage, protected by a "shadow" or "heavens" or roof, is entered by two doors; behind the doors is the "tiring house" (attiring house, i.e., dressing room), and above the doors is some sort of gallery that may sometimes hold spectators but that can be used (for example) as the bedroom from which Romeo —according to a stage direction in one text—"goeth down." Some evidence suggests that a throne can be lowered onto the platform stage, perhaps from the "shadow"; certainly characters can descend from the stage through a trap or traps into the cellar or "hell." Sometimes this space beneath the platform accommodates a sound-effects man or musician (in *Antony and Cleopatra* "music of the hautboys is under the stage") or an actor (in *Hamlet* the "Ghost cries under the stage"). Most characters simply walk on and off, but because there is no curtain in front of the platform, corpses will have to be carried off (Hamlet must lug Polonius' guts into the neighbor room), or will have to fall at the rear, where the curtain on the alcove or booth can be drawn to conceal them.

Such may have been the so-called "public theater." Another kind of theater, called the "private theater" because its much greater admission charge limited its audience to the wealthy or the prodigal, must be briefly mentioned. The private theater was basically a large room, entirely roofed and therefore artificially illuminated, with a stage at one end. In 1576 one such theater was established in Blackfriars, a Dominican priory in London that had been suppressed in 1538 and confiscated by the Crown and thus was not under the city's jurisdiction. All the actors in the Blackfriars theater were boys about eight to thirteen years old (in the public theaters similar boys played female parts; a boy Lady Macbeth played to a man Macbeth). This private theater had a precarious existence, and ceased operations in 1584. In 1596 James Burbage, who had already made theatrical history by building the Theater, began to construct a second Black-friars theater. He died in 1597, and for several years this second Blackfriars theater was used by a troupe of boys, but in 1608 two of Burbage's sons and five other actors (including Shakespeare) became joint operators of the theater, using it in the winter when the open-air Globe was unsuitable. Perhaps such a smaller theater, roofed, artificially illuminated, and with a tradition of a courtly audience, exerted an influence on Shakespeare's late plays.

Performances in the private theaters may well have had intermissions during which music was played, but in the public theaters the action was probably uninterrupted, flowing from scene to scene almost without a break. Actors would enter, speak, exit, and others would immediately enter and establish (if necessary) the new locale by a few properties and by words and gestures. Here are some samples of Shakespeare's scene painting:

> This is Illyria, lady.

> Well, this is the Forest of Arden.

> This castle hath a pleasant seat; the air
> Nimbly and sweetly recommends itself
> Unto our gentle senses.

On the other hand, it is a mistake to conceive of the Elizabethan stage as bare. Although Shakespeare's Chorus in *Henry V* calls the stage an "unworthy scaffold" and urges the spectators to "eke out our performance with your mind," there was considerable spectacle. The last

act of *Macbeth,* for example, has five stage directions
calling for "drum and colors," and another sort of appeal
to the eye is indicated by the stage direction "Enter Mac-
duff, with Macbeth's head." Some scenery and properties
may have been substantial; doubtless a throne was used,
and in one play of the period we encounter this direction:
"Hector takes up a great piece of rock and casts at Ajax,
who tears up a young tree by the roots and assails Hector." The matter is of some importance, and will be
glanced at again in the next section.

The Texts of Shakespeare

Though eighteen of his plays were published during his
lifetime, Shakespeare seems never to have supervised their
publication. There is nothing unusual here; when a playwright sold a play to a theatrical company he surrendered
his ownership of it. Normally a company would not publish the play, because to publish it meant to allow com-
petitors to acquire the piece. Some plays, however, did get
published: apparently treacherous actors sometimes
pieced together a play for a publisher, sometimes a company in need of money sold a play, and sometimes a
company allowed a play to be published that no longer
drew audiences. That Shakespeare did not concern himself with publication, then, is scarcely remarkable; of his
contemporaries only Ben Jonson carefully supervised the
publication of his own plays. In 1623, seven years after
Shakespeare's death, John Heminges and Henry Condell
(two senior members of Shakespeare's company, who
had performed with him for about twenty years) collected his plays—published and unpublished—into a large
volume, commonly called the First Folio. (A folio is a
volume consisting of sheets that have been folded
once, each sheet thus making two leaves, or four pages.
The eighteen plays published during Shakespeare's lifetime had been issued one play per volume in small books
called quartos. Each sheet in a quarto has been folded
twice, making four leaves, or eight pages.) The First

Folio contains thirty-six plays; a thirty-seventh, *Pericles,* though not in the Folio is regarded as canonical. Hemings and Condell suggest in an address "To the great variety of readers" that the republished plays are presented in better form than in the quartos: "Before you were abused with diverse stolen and surreptitious copies, maimed and deformed by the frauds and stealths of injurious impostors that exposed them; even those, are now offered to your view cured and perfect of their limbs, and all the rest absolute in their numbers, as he [i.e., Shakespeare] conceived them."

Whoever was assigned to prepare the texts for publication in the First Folio seems to have taken his job seriously and yet not to have performed it with uniform care. The sources of the texts seem to have been, in general, good unpublished copies or the best published copies. The first play in the collection, *The Tempest,* is divided into acts and scenes, has unusually full stage directions and descriptions of spectacle, and concludes with a list of the characters, but the editor was not able (or willing) to present all of the succeeding texts so fully dressed. Later texts occasionally show signs of carelessness: in one scene of *Much Ado About Nothing* the names of actors, instead of characters, appear as speech prefixes, as they had in the quarto, which the Folio reprints; proofreading throughout the Folio is spotty and apparently was done without reference to the printer's copy; the pagination of *Hamlet* jumps from 156 to 257.

A modern editor of Shakespeare must first select his copy; no problem if the play exists only in the Folio, but a considerable problem if the relationship between a quarto and the Folio—or an early quarto and a later one —is unclear. When an editor has chosen what seems to him to be the most authoritative text or texts for his copy, he has not done with making decisions. First of all, he must reckon with Elizabethan spelling. If he is not producing a facsimile, he probably modernizes it, but ought he to preserve the old form of words that apparently were pronounced quite unlike their modern forms—"lanthorn," "alablaster"? If he preserves these forms, is he really preserving Shakespeare's forms or perhaps those of a compositor in the printing house? What is one to do when one finds "lanthorn" and "lantern" in adjacent lines? (The editors of this series in general, but not invariably, assume that words should be spelled in their modern form.) Elizabethan punctuation, too, presents problems. For example in the First Folio, the only text for the play, Macbeth rejects his wife's idea that he can wash the blood from his hand:

> no: this my Hand will rather
> The multitudinous Seas incarnardine,
> Making the Greene one, Red.

Obviously an editor will remove the superfluous capitals, and he will probably alter the spelling to "incarnadine," but will he leave the comma before "red," letting Macbeth speak of the sea as "the green one," or will he (like most modern editors) remove the comma and thus have Macbeth say that his hand will make the ocean *uniformly* red?

An editor will sometimes have to change more than spelling or punctuation. Macbeth says to his wife:

> I dare do all that may become a man,
> Who dares no more, is none.

For two centuries editors have agreed that the second line is unsatisfactory, and have emended "no" to "do": "Who dares do more is none." But when in the same play Ross says that fearful persons

> floate vpon a wilde and violent Sea
> Each way, and moue,

need "move" be emended to "none," as it often is, on the hunch that the compositor misread the manuscript? The editors of the Signet Classic Shakespeare have restrained themselves from making abundant emendations.

In their minds they hear Dr. Johnson on the dangers of emending: "I have adopted the Roman sentiment, that it is more honorable to save a citizen than to kill an enemy." Some departures (in addition to spelling, punctuation, and lineation) from the copy text have of course been made, but the original readings are listed in a note following the play, so that the reader can evaluate them for himself.

The editors of the Signet Classic Shakespeare, following tradition, have added line numbers and in many cases act and scene divisions as well as indications of locale at the beginning of scenes. The Folio divided most of the plays into acts and some into scenes. Early eighteenth-century editors increased the divisions. These divisions, which provide a convenient way of referring to passages in the plays, have been retained, but when not in the text chosen as the basis for the Signet Classic text they are enclosed in square brackets [ ] to indicate that they are editorial additions. Similarly, although no play of Shakespeare's published during his lifetime was equipped with indications of locale at the heads of scene divisions, locales have here been added in square brackets for the convenience of the reader, who lacks the information afforded to spectators by costumes, properties, and gestures. The spectator can tell at a glance he is in the throne room, but without an editorial indication the reader may be puzzled for a while. It should be mentioned, incidentally, that there are a few authentic stage directions—perhaps Shakespeare's, perhaps a prompter's—that suggest locales: for example, "Enter Brutus in his orchard," and "They go up into the Senate house." It is hoped that the bracketed additions provide the reader with the sort of help provided in these two authentic directions, but it is equally hoped that the reader will remember that the stage was not loaded with scenery.

No editor during the course of his work can fail to recollect some words Heminges and Condell prefixed to the Folio:

It had been a thing, we confess, worthy to have been wished, that the author himself had lived to have set forth and overseen his own writings. But since it hath been ordained otherwise, and he by death departed from that right, we pray you do not envy his friends the office of their care and pain to have collected and published them.

Nor can an editor, after he has done his best, forget Heminges and Condell's final words: "And so we leave you to other of his friends, whom if you need can be your guides. If you need them not, you can lead yourselves, and others. And such readers we wish him."

SYLVAN BARNET
Tufts University

Introduction

A study of Shakespeare's development as a dramatic artist shows that one of his supreme achievements during his "middle period" consists in combining heterogeneous elements in a single play. The dramas of Shakespeare's predecessors all exist on a smaller scale, mostly adhering to one particular type and keeping within more limited resources of style and subject matter. However, even in his very first comedies, *The Two Gentlemen of Verona, The Comedy of Errors,* and *Love's Labor's Lost,* we see Shakespeare widening the scope of the dramatic genre to which these plays belong and introducing new elements taken over from other sections of the literary tradition of the past. *A Midsummer Night's Dream,* then, which must have been written about 1595, combines for the first time totally disparate worlds into one unified whole; the sharp contrasts brought together there would have destroyed the play's balance in the hands of any lesser playwright. For, indeed, it required Shakespeare's genius to bring together Bottom and Puck, the crude realism of the artisans and the exquisite delicacy of the fairy world, the stylized and pointed repartee of the Athenian lovers and the dignified manner of Theseus and Hippolyta. What we find are contrasts on many levels, exemplified by diversified means. Yet Shakespeare strikes an equilibrium between these contrasts, reconciling and fusing the discordant factors within the organic body of his comedy. *A Midsummer Night's Dream,* therefore, not only exhibits bold contrasts and divergent elements of plot, atmosphere, and character; it also illustrates the unifying power of the spirit of comedy and the poetic imagination. We further find that the play's unity is reinforced by a subtle technique of counterpoint and juxtaposition, a skillful contrasting of different strands of plot, and the creation of an atmosphere full of illusion, wonder, and strangeness, all of which facilitate the many transitions occurring during the course of the play.

Some facts about its origin and title may help us better to understand the particular nature of the play. *A Midsummer Night's Dream* is clearly related to the practices of midsummer night, the night before June 24, which was the date of St. John the Baptist's festival and hence connected with merrymaking, various superstitions and folk customs, dances, pageants, and revels. More than any other night in the year, midsummer night suggested enchantment and witchcraft, something which Shakespeare has superbly embodied in his fairy world. To an Elizabethan audience, moreover, the play's title would have immediately called to mind the so-called "midsummer madness," which was a state of mind marked by a heightened readiness to believe in the delusions of the imagination that were thought to befall the minds of men after days of great summer heat. Thus, by means of his highly suggestive title, Shakespeare has firmly planted the dreamlike action of his drama in the popular beliefs and customs of his time. Furthermore the title gives theatergoers and readers a clue as to how the work should be understood—namely, as an unrealistic creation of the imagination, a series of dream images containing all the contradictions and inconsistencies that dreams normally possess, but containing too their symbolic content. Indeed, the dreamlike character of what takes place is repeatedly alluded to. In Puck's epilogue, for instance, the audience themselves are explicitly addressed:

> And this weak and idle theme,
> No more yielding but a dream,
> Gentles, do not reprehend . . .

In short, the play's title makes significant allusion to the nature and meaning of the work, though it makes no reference to the period of time during which the events of the drama occur. In fact, the action takes place between April 29 and May 1, the latter date, being that of May Day, demanding of course particular celebrations, and for that reason it is perhaps a suitable day for the marriage of Theseus and Hippolyta.

Now the wedding of the princely pair is not only the destination of the action; it is also the occasion for which the play itself was written. *A Midsummer Night's Dream* was undoubtedly intended as a dramatic epithalamium to celebrate the marriage of some aristocratic couple. (The attempts made to fix on a definite historical marriage, however, must remain conjectural.) Plays written for such festive occasions addressed themselves to an aristocratic audience. They were mostly performed on private stages rather than in public theaters and revealed an entirely different style of performance from the popular dramas. The relationship of *A Midsummer Night's Dream* to the court masque—something which Act V, Scene i, line 40 draws attention to—also comes in here. The masques formed a central part of the entertainments that were always given at court celebrations, and several noticeable features in *A Midsummer Night's Dream* clearly relate to the genre of the court masque. The music and dances, the appearance of fairylike creatures possessed of supernatural qualities, the employment of motifs involving magic and metamorphosis, and the vigorous stylization and symmetrical structure of some parts do indeed remind one of the court masque. Finally, the scenes with Bottom, Quince, and company may be compared to the anti-masque, which formed the burlesque and realistic counterpart performed together with the masque itself.

In referring to the masque, one is only pointing out a single aspect of *A Midsummer Night's Dream*. We must also remember that Shakespeare has similarly taken over stylistic and formal elements from his own early comedies, popular drama, the romantic play, and the mythological dream plays of John Lyly. Shakespeare has tapped many sources, but he has nevertheless been able to create an original and independent form of drama that includes skillful organization of plot—involving the manipulation of three subplots that run parallel to one another—as well as a rich suffusion of the whole by both the atmosphere of nature and that of magic. Between a descriptive and retrospective kind of dramatic method and one that makes us see the process of things in action Shakespeare has struck a perfect sense of balance.

A study of the interrelation of the four plots reveals how their contrasts, juxtapositions, and dovetailing help to disclose the meaning of the drama. The play begins with a scene between Theseus and Hippolyta, who do not appear again until Act IV. In Act V their wedding is celebrated. The plot involving Theseus and Hippolyta can therefore be styled an "enveloping action" that provides the play with a definite framework and a firmly established temporal scaffolding; it stands outside the world of dream, enchantment, and love entanglements, suggesting the sphere of everyday reality out of which the events of the drama first develop and to which they then ultimately return. The section in Scene i with Egeus, Hermia, Lysander, and Demetrius relates the Theseus-Hippolyta plot to that of the lovers, for Theseus himself appears as arbitrator in the love dispute and it will be on his wedding day that the harsh verdict he passes on Hermia is to take effect, should she not have changed her mind by that date. This verdict is the cause of Hermia and Lysander's decision to flee into the wood near Athens, so that with this the events of the second and third acts have already been determined. The comic subplot, moreover, beginning in Scene ii with the gathering of the artisans to prepare themselves for rehearsal, is also announced in Scene i, insofar as we learn of the entertainments to be presented on Theseus' wedding day. Theseus' promise to woo Hippolyta "With pomp, with triumph, and with reveling" can also be understood as an allusion to the dramatic entertainments that are to come later. From the very beginning, then, our expectations are raised in connection with

the wedding day, which is to bring with it the artisans' play, the decision regarding the love dispute between the Athenian couples, and the festive marriage of Theseus and Hippolyta.

If this were all that Shakespeare had given us, we would have had a comedy little different from his early ones. The plot connected with the fairies, however, with Oberon and Titania at its center, not only brings considerable complications into the course of the above-mentioned matters, but also adds to the whole drama a new feature that Shakespeare had never employed before. For the supernatural, which intervenes in the activities of the characters, turns their intentions upside down, and directs their actions. It is the fairies who are responsible for the confusion, and also for the final reconciliation, thus substituting enchantment and arbitrariness for the lovers' own responsibility and power of will. Yet these influences also have repercussions on the fairies themselves, because Titania thereby falls in love with the ass-headed Bottom. Thus the world of the fairies is linked with that of the artisans, and we get those incomparably comic situations that are themselves the outcome of the fairies' intervention. Finally, a link between the plots dealing with the fairies and Theseus emerges in the conversation between Oberon and Titania in which the fairy rulers' earlier connections with Theseus and Hippolyta are recalled; and this is a moment that accelerates the pair's mutual jealousy and estrangement.

Since the fairies remain always invisible to the other members of the *dramatis personae* (only Bottom is ironically allowed the privilege of seeing Titania), and their deeds are accomplished without the knowledge of the other characters, Shakespeare has been able to achieve a highly dramatic effect of "double awareness." We as audience are aware of Puck's magic juice and therefore look forward with pleasure to what might develop. We know even more than the usually omniscient Oberon, who does not realize till some time later the confusion that Puck has caused by mistake. This error on Puck's part bears deeper significance, for it shows that even the fairies can err and

that the influences they exert as supernatural agents in the play do not in the least answer to anything providential, but rather contain filaments of arbitrariness, self-deception, and folly.

An insight into the peculiar nature of the fairy world in *A Midsummer Night's Dream* helps us to understand the entire play, for although the fairies certainly possess supernatural qualities, they are nevertheless closely linked to the world of mankind and have their share of human frailties. Their origin in the realm of the elemental and their partly instinctive, partly playful nature, together with their capriciousness and irrationality, indicate which forces and qualities Shakespeare wanted us to see as conditioning and influencing human love relationships; for the haphazard and arbitrary game that love plays with the two Athenian couples appears as a projection of the irrationality, irresponsibility, and playfulness characterizing the nature of the fairies themselves. However, the fairies not only make other people behave in a way that corresponds, as it were, to their own fairy natures; they also strengthen and reinforce people's latent tendencies. Previous to the fairies' intervention, we learn from Demetrius that he has loved Helena before bestowing his affections on Hermia (I.i.106–07, 242–43); it is not for nothing that he is termed "spotted and inconstant man" (I.i.110).

Shakespeare has interspersed his text with numerous illuminating hints referring to the fairies' peculiar traits of character and sphere of existence, so that we are able to get a vivid picture of the type of creatures they are. Although the world of the fairies exhibits several characteristics common to popular belief and folklore tradition, it is to a considerable extent a new creation of Shakespeare's own. This is particularly true when we think of Puck, whose descent from Robin Goodfellow or Hobgoblin, as he is called by one of the fairies when he first appears (II.i.34,40), only accounts for one aspect of his being. If one examines the numerous statements that Puck utters about himself and that the other characters utter about him, one immediately realizes that Shakespeare

has created a complex dramatic figure to whom is assigned a key position within the fabric of the play. Not only is Puck the comically rough and earth-bound goblin with his mischievous pranks, blunt speech, and intervention in day-to-day affairs; he is also a spirit closely linked with the elements, having command over supernatural powers and capable of moving at incredible speed. As "Oberon's jester" he is close to the fools of Shakespeare's later comedies, enjoying his own jests and possessing the gift of sharp, critical observation. Keeping this last point in mind, we see that Shakespeare has assigned him the role of spectator several times during the course of the play, and as such he comments on the action and aptly characterizes the people taking part. Hence it is he who, in view of the confusion he has caused among the lovers, cries out:

> Shall we their fond pageant see?
> Lord, what fools these mortals be!

> (III.ii.114–15)

Thus Puck becomes the interpreter of the play's dramatic situations and intermediary between stage and audience as he places himself at a distance from events that have depended on and been influenced by him, and to which in the epilogue, significantly spoken by him, he is able to look back, as from a higher vantage point. Indeed, it is remarkable how many motives determining the play's action derive from Puck, how many invisible wires he holds in his hand. Yet his interventions in the development of the plot are as much the result of a casual mood or mischievous whim as they are the result of premeditated instructions from his master, Oberon. This is shown, for instance, in the case of Bottom's transformation in the first scene of Act III. It is a paradox of the dramatic action that Oberon's well-meaning intention is turned into its opposite through Puck's mistake (Lysander, instead of Demetrius, is anointed with the magic herb), so that the activity of the supernatural forces seems to be largely conditioned by error and coincidence. Still, it is precisely this fickleness and inconstancy of fate that Puck acknowledges in his laconic answer to Oberon when the latter reproves him for the mistake: "Then fate o'errules . . ." With these words Puck gives utterance to a basic motif in the drama.

It has often been stressed that in *A Midsummer Night's Dream* Shakespeare wanted to portray the irrational nature of love, the shifting and unstable "fancy" that continually falls prey to illusion, regards itself as being playful and short-lived, and is accompanied by a certain irresponsibility; whereas in *Romeo and Juliet,* written during the same period, love appears in quite a different shape, as a fateful and all-consuming force making claims to absolute authority and demanding that the whole of the self be yielded up to it.

But Shakespeare makes clear to us in several ways that the love between the Athenian couples is not rooted in actuality. Puck's magic juice, operating as a supernatural medium, is of course only one of the means by which Shakespeare places the relationships of the four Athenian lovers outside of reality. The love entanglements occur during a night full of dreams and enchantment, of which only an imprecise picture afterward remains in the memory of those concerned. Furthermore, it is undoubtedly the poet's deliberate intention (contrary to his practice in other plays of the same period) that the lovers should be so weakly characterized that it is impossible for us to retain them in our memory as real and differentiated human beings. We may likewise take it for granted that their symmetrical grouping and their appearance in pairs is the result of conscious stylization on Shakespeare's part. And if the style of their dialogues, together with the handling of the verse, often seems to be flat, trite, and frankly silly, this neither signifies Shakespeare's lack of skill nor justifies the contention that passages have been left in from an earlier version of the same play. Rather it gives evidence that Shakespeare intended the four lovers to be just what they are, puppets and not fully realized characters. Even the spectator to those scenes of confusion in the wood soon has no idea where he is or who precisely is in love with whom.

Above all, however, the dreamlike atmosphere of such

scenes accentuates our feeling that the four lovers appear
to be quite removed from any criteria applicable to reality. "The willing suspension of disbelief" that Coleridge
designated as one of the poet's chief aims Shakespeare
achieves by creating a world of illusion that manifests
itself from the first scene onward. Dream world and reality merge imperceptibly, so that the persons concerned
are not sure themselves in which sphere they move, nor
whether what they have experienced has been imagination or truth. The idea that what has happened has
been a dream, illusion, or "vision" is often expressed
from various standpoints by the characters themselves.
"Dream" is a key word in the drama, and the idea that
everything is based on imagination is given frequent and
subtle variation. The art with which Shakespeare shifts
from the dream world to reality is unique. This is evident
in the first scene of Act IV, where both the lovers and
Bottom are depicted as awaking out of their dreams—a
scene in which all four plots are brought together for the
first time, whereby the mind of the spectator is made to
see the boundaries separating them as being simultane-
ously nonexistent and yet firmly fixed. Finally, as if in a
series of flashbacks, the incidents that have occurred during the night of dreams are lit up once again from a distance by means of Theseus' famous speech describing
"the lunatic, the lover, and the poet" as being "of imagination all compact." These words refer once more to that
faculty which lies behind not only dreams, but the poet's
own creations as well and under whose spell we, as spectators, have been kept during the whole course of the
play; for we too have been enchanted, responding eagerly
to the call of the poetry and accepting the play as an
organism that conforms to its own rules, a world where
strange and real things mingle in a curious way.

   The illusion of a dream sequence scurrying past is also
enhanced by a sense of the forward surge of time. Not
only is the passing of night into morning given expression
through the shifting movement of light and dark within a
series of superb images and subtle allusions: the impa-
tience and longing with which the different characters

look forward to the future are perceptible from the very start, thus making time flow in an anticipatory way. Again, the language of the play is rich in images and expressions indicating quick movement, lightness, and transitoriness, thereby contributing to the over-all atmospheric impression. How delicately and accurately the play's particular atmosphere, together with its theme and leitmotifs, is rendered from the very beginning, an examination of the first scene of the play alone would show, although we can permit ourselves only a few observations here.

The very first exchange between Theseus and Hippolyta conveys to us a twofold awareness of time, from the standpoint of which we contemplate a time span that culminates in the wedding day, the date of which is fixed immediately at the outset. This emerges when Hippolyta's "Four days will quickly steep themselves in night;/ Four nights will quickly dream away the time" is contrasted with Theseus' ". . . but, O, methinks, how slow/ This old moon wanes!" During this initial dialogue Shakespeare skillfully puts us in tune with the moonlit scenes that follow by means of Theseus' comparison of the "old moon" with "a stepdame, or a dowager/ Long withering out a young man's revenue." In this scene alone "moon" and "night" each occur five times, "dream" three times. The lines just quoted also suggest the aristocratic world of the court, where a part of the action is to take place. A further element is introduced when, immediately following, we read these instructions to Philostrate:

> Stir up the Athenian youth to merriments,
> Awake the pert and nimble spirit of mirth. . . .

Yet the entry of Egeus immediately afterward, leading in his daughter Hermia and, "full of vexation," bringing accusations against Lysander because the latter "hath bewitched the bosom of [his] child," ushers in the radically contrasting note of discord, deception, and trickery, something that is never missing in any Shakespearean comedy and is always present as an undercurrent in *A Midsum-*

mer Night's Dream; for the final state of harmony reached at the end of the play both in the world of the fairies and that of the court turns out to be a resolution of previously opposed forces, a reconciliation attained after former estrangement, and "the concord of this discord" (V.i.60).

The main theme of the drama—namely, the transitoriness and inconstancy of love—is also anticipated in this first scene when Lysander describes love as

> . . . momentany as a sound,
> Swift as a shadow, short as any dream,
> Brief as the lightning in the collied night,
> That, in a spleen, unfolds both heaven and earth,
> And ere a man hath power to say "Behold!"
> The jaws of darkness do devour it up:
> So quick bright things come to confusion.

> (I.i.143–49)

This passage is illuminating because it shows how Shakespeare not only bodies forth the themes and motifs of his drama in terms of action, but also gives them expression through imagery. In no other play of Shakespeare's middle period do we find so much poetry and verse melody, or indeed nature imagery, with its references to plants, animals, and other natural phenomena; nature itself even enters the drama as a participating agent alongside the characters. *A Midsummer Night's Dream* should therefore be apprehended as poetry and music, and not only be absorbed and endorsed by the eye and intellect as a connected series of actions. For the play's language, by means of its images, its subtle allusions and suggestions, its verbal repetitions and rhythmic patterns, has built up a complex and finely varied tissue of ideas, impressions, and associations that constantly act on our powers of imagination and stimulate them to participate. The great range and delicacy of impact that poetic drama possesses, as opposed to prose drama, can be perfectly witnessed in *A Midsummer Night's Dream.*

The degree to which the language, with its proliferation of allusions, ironies, and ambiguities, creates the over-all dramatic effect is made clear by those prose scenes with the artisans, where the lyrical and poetic are completely lacking. Apart from suggesting a wealth of gestures, the language used by Bottom and company is rich in implications and evokes delightful misunderstandings; it gives expression to the artisans' ludicrous ambition for higher things as well as to their rustic limitations. All this gives rise to that constant incongruity which is the prerequisite for great comedy—the incongruity existing between the basic natures of the characters and their pretensions. The scenes with Bottom, Quince, and company provide a comic and realistic contrast to the poetry of the fairies and the artificial and stylized love scenes of the Athenians. Thus the delicacy, polished bearing, and lightness inherent in all other sections of the play are counterbalanced by the uncouthness, the heavy solidity of everyday life, and a naïve roughness that the artisans bring into the magical fairy world of the moonlit scenes. Puck, the shrewd onlooker, at one stage justly calls them "hempen homespuns." But Shakespeare has made far more out of this antimasque than a merely amusing subplot filled with clownlike figures; during the course of the play one of them has come to be the most unforgettable character in the entire drama. For the lack of vitality and pronounced individuality noticeable in the other personages we are fully recompensed in Bottom, who has justly been described as the greatest comic creation in the dramatist's early work. Abundantly endowed with remarkable qualities, Bottom is continually putting himself in a comic light. There are no features of his character that at one point or another do not lead to some ridiculous situation, some unforgettable moment of contrast or unintentionally provoked comparison. Bottom's supreme satisfaction with himself and his sense of ease remain with him even in his transformed state, while his stage ambitions (he wants to play the part of the lion as well as that of Pyramus, Thisby and the tyrant) parody the profession of acting and yet at the same time form a characteristic trait that fits him remarkably well. That his ambitions are fulfilled even before the Pyramus and Thisby drama takes place, insofar as Bottom has to play the parts of both ass and lover, is significant, just as is the marked irony that Bottom alone, out of all the persons in the play, is permitted to come into contact with the fairies—though this encounter does not impress him in the least or signify for him any unusual experience. In Titania's presence he discards nothing at all of his own personality; the ass's head, which with other people would have resulted in monstrous caricature, in his case is something that illuminates for us his real nature.

If the story of the craftsmen forms a satirical counterbalance to the plot of the lovers, then it is also true to say that the drama of Pyramus and Thisby initiates a twofold, even threefold kind of awareness. For what we get in this parody of the love tragedy is an exaggerated depiction of the four lovers' sentimentality, their highflown protestations of love, and their pseudo-solemnity—a depiction in the form of a flashback that they themselves are now able to contemplate as spectators, serenely calm and reconciled with one another. The lovers' own relationships have likewise been a play that the fairies have found highly amusing, and these entanglements parallel the quarrel between Oberon and Titania, the quarrel from which the confusion among the lovers originated.

"The play within the play," superbly worked out by Shakespeare, makes us particularly aware that the entire drama has indeed been a "play," summoned into life by the dramatist's magic wand and just as easily made to vanish. When Puck refers in the first line of his epilogue ("If we shadows have offended") not merely to the fairies, previously termed "shadows," but also to all the actors who have taken part, we realize that Shakespeare is once more making it clear to us that we have been watching a "magic-lantern show," something where appearance, not reality, is the operative factor.

It is peculiarly ironic that Bottom, Quince, and company perform the tragedy of Pyramus and Thisby as an auspicious offering on behalf of the newly established love union, thereby, one might say, presenting the material of

Romeo and Juliet in a comic and grotesque manner. Thus an exaggerated form of tragedy is employed so that the preceding scenes may be parodied as comedy. The play of Pyramus and Thisby parodies not only the torments of love, which the Athenian lovers can now look back on with serene calmness, but also the Senecan style of Elizabethan tragedy with its melodrama and ponderous conventions. Shakespeare parodies these conventions here by means of exaggeration or clumsy and grotesque usage— the too explicit prologue, for instance; the verbose self-explanation and commentaries; the stereotyped phrases for expressing grief; and the excessive use of such rhetorical devices as apostrophe, alliteration, hyperbole, and rhetorical question.

Even the elements of comedy and parody in the Pyramus and Thisby performance appear in a twofold light. Though they themselves are being mocked, the lovers smile at these awkward efforts on the part of the craftsmen, and Theseus even adds a highly suggestive commentary.

In the craftsmen's play, Shakespeare is also parodying the whole life of the theater. He calmly takes the shortcomings of all theatrical production and acting, drives them to absurd lengths, and holds them up for inspection. The lantern, which is supposed to represent the moon, makes us conscious of how equally inadequate Pyramus and Thisby are in their roles and suggests that such inadequacy may time and again have made its appearance on the Elizabethan stage. For those Elizabethan playgoers who viewed a play superficially, without using their own powers of imagination, much in Shakespearean drama must have remained completely unintelligible. It is at such narrow-minded theatergoers as these that Shakespeare is indirectly poking fun. And he enables us to see the limitations of his own stage, which had to portray a large world and create atmosphere without the elaborate scenery and technical equipment that we have today.

But the very inadequacy of the artisans' production gives emphasis to the true art of dramatic illusion and magic, as we have witnessed it in the preceding scenes, in which the evocative power of Shakespeare's language, assisted by our imagination, enables us to experience moonlight and nighttime in the woods. Theseus himself makes this point when, in answer to Hippolyta's remark, "This is the silliest stuff that ever I heard," he says: "The best in this kind are but shadows; and the worst are no worse, if imagination amend them."

WOLFGANG CLEMEN
University of Munich

The editor wishes to express his thanks to Dr. Dieter Mehl for assistance in the compilation of the notes.

A Midsummer Night's Dream

[*Dramatis Personae*

Theseus, Duke of Athens
Egeus, father to Hermia
Lysander } in love with Hermia
Demetrius }
Philostrate, Master of the Revels to Theseus
Peter Quince, a carpenter; Prologue in the play
Snug, a joiner; Lion in the play
Nick Bottom, a weaver; Pyramus in the play
Francis Flute, a bellows mender; Thisby in the play
Tom Snout, a tinker; Wall in the play
Robin Starveling, a tailor; Moonshine in the play
Hippolyta, Queen of the Amazons, betrothed to Theseus
Hermia, daughter to Egeus, in love with Lysander
Helena, in love with Demetrius
Oberon, King of the Fairies
Titania, Queen of the Fairies
Puck, or Robin Goodfellow
Peaseblossom }
Cobweb }
Moth } fairies
Mustardseed }
Other Fairies attending their King and Queen
Attendants on Theseus and Hippolyta

Scene: Athens, and a wood near it]

- nobles usually speak in blank verse
- lovers usually speak in rhymed couplets
- rustics speak in prose
A Midsummer Night's Dream
- faeries speak in lyric poetry

[ACT I]

Scene I. *The palace of Theseus.*]

Enter Theseus, Hippolyta, [Philostrate,] with others.

Theseus. Now, fair Hippolyta, our nuptial hour
  Draws on apace. Four happy days bring in
  Another moon; but, O, methinks, how slow
  This old moon wanes! She lingers°¹ my desires,
  Like to a stepdame, or a dowager,   5
  Long withering out a young man's revenue.°

Hippolyta. Four days will quickly steep themselves in night,
  Four nights will quickly dream away the time;
  And then the moon, like to a silver bow
  New-bent in heaven, shall behold the night   10
  Of our solemnities.

Theseus.   Go, Philostrate,
  Stir up the Athenian youth to merriments,
  Awake the pert° and nimble spirit of mirth,
  Turn melancholy forth to funerals;

¹ The degree signs (°) indicates a footnote, which is keyed to the text by line number. Text references are printed in *italic* type; the annotation follows in roman type.
I.i. 4 *lingers* makes to linger, delays   6 *Long withering out a young man's revenue* diminishing the young man's money (because she must be supported by him)   13 *pert* lively

15   The pale companion° is not for our pomp.°

[*Exit Philostrate.*]

Hippolyta, I wooed thee with my sword,°
And won thy love, doing thee injuries;
But I will wed thee in another key,
With pomp, with triumph, and with reveling.

*Enter Egeus and his daughter Hermia, and Lysander,
and Demetrius.*

20   *Egeus.* Happy be Theseus, our renownèd Duke!

Theseus. Thanks, good Egeus.° What's the news with
thee?

Egeus. Full of vexation come I, with complaint
Against my child, my daughter Hermia.
Stand forth, Demetrius. My noble lord,
25   This man hath my consent to marry her.
Stand forth, Lysander. And, my gracious Duke
This man hath bewitched the bosom of my child.
Thou, thou, Lysander, thou hast given her rhymes,
And interchanged love tokens with my child.
30   Thou hast by moonlight at her window sung,
With feigning voice, verses of feigning love,
And stol'n the impression of her fantasy°
With bracelets of thy hair, rings, gauds, conceits,
Knacks,° trifles, nosegays, sweetmeats, messengers
35   Of strong prevailment in unhardened youth.
With cunning hast thou filched my daughter's heart,
Turned her obedience, which is due to me,
To stubborn harshness. And, my gracious Duke,
Be it so she will not here before your Grace
40   Consent to marry with Demetrius,
I beg the ancient privilege of Athens:

15 *companion* fellow (contemptuous)   15 *pomp* festive procession
16 *I wooed thee with my sword* (Theseus had captured Hippolyta
when he conquered the Amazons)   21 *Egeus* (pronounced "E-gé-
us")   32 *stol'n the impression of her fantasy* fraudulently impressed
your image upon her imagination   33–34 *gauds, conceits, Knacks*
trinkets, cleverly devised tokens, knickknacks

As she is mine, I may dispose of her,
Which shall be either to this gentleman
Or to her death, according to our law
Immediately° provided in that case.   45

Theseus. What say you, Hermia? Be advised, fair
    maid.
To you your father should be as a god,
One that composed your beauties; yea, and one
To whom you are but as a form in wax
By him imprinted and within his power   50
To leave the figure or disfigure it.
Demetrius is a worthy gentleman.

Hermia. So is Lysander.

Theseus.   In himself he is;
But in this kind, wanting your father's voice,°
The other must be held the worthier.   55

Hermia. I would my father looked but with my eyes.

Theseus. Rather your eyes must with his judgment
    look.

Hermia. I do entreat your Grace to pardon me.
I know not by what power I am made bold,
Nor how it may concern my modesty,   60
In such a presence here to plead my thoughts;
But I beseech your Grace that I may know
The worst that may befall me in this case,
If I refuse to wed Demetrius.

Theseus. Either to die the death, or to abjure   65
Forever the society of men.
Therefore, fair Hermia, question your desires;
Know of° your youth, examine well your blood,°
Whether, if you yield not to your father's choice,
You can endure the livery of a nun,   70
For aye to be in shady cloister mewed,°
To live a barren sister all your life,

45 *Immediately* expressly   54 *But in . . . father's voice* but in this
particular respect, lacking your father's approval   68 *Know of*
ascertain from   68 *blood* passions   71 *mewed* caged

Chanting faint hymns to the cold fruitless moon.°
Thrice-blessèd they that master so their blood,
75 To undergo such maiden pilgrimage;
But earthlier happy is the rose distilled,°
Than that which, withering on the virgin thorn,
Grows, lives, and dies in single blessedness.

Hermia. So will I grow, so live, so die, my lord,
80 Ere I will yield my virgin patent° up
Unto his lordship, whose unwished yoke
My soul consents not to give sovereignty.

Theseus. Take time to pause; and, by the next new
    moon—
The sealing day betwixt my love and me,
85 For everlasting bond of fellowship—
Upon that day either prepare to die
For disobedience to your father's will,
Or else to wed Demetrius, as he would,
Or on Diana's altar to protest
90 For aye austerity and single life.

Demetrius. Relent, sweet Hermia: and, Lysander,
    yield
Thy crazèd title° to my certain right.

Lysander. You have her father's love, Demetrius;
Let me have Hermia's: do you marry him.

95 *Egeus.* Scornful Lysander! True, he hath my love,
And what is mine my love shall render him.
And she is mine, and all my right of her
I do estate unto° Demetrius.

Lysander. I am, my lord, as well derived as he,
100 As well possessed;° my love is more than his;
My fortunes every way as fairly ranked
(If not with vantage°) as Demetrius';
And, which is more than all these boasts can be,

73 *moon* i.e., Diana, goddess of chastity   76 *distilled* made into
perfumes   80 *patent* privilege   92 *crazed title* flawed claim   98 *estate unto* settle upon   100 *As well possessed* as rich   102 *If not
with vantage* if not better

I am beloved of beauteous Hermia.
Why should not I then prosecute my right?   105
Demetrius, I'll avouch it to his head,°
Made love to Nedar's daughter, Helena,
And won her soul; and she, sweet lady, dotes,
Devoutly dotes, dotes in idolatry,
Upon this spotted° and inconstant man.   110

Theseus. I must confess that I have heard so much,
And with Demetrius thought to have spoke thereof;
But, being overfull of self-affairs,
My mind did lose it. But, Demetrius, come;
And come, Egeus. You shall go with me;   115
I have some private schooling for you both.
For you, fair Hermia, look you arm yourself
To fit your fancies to your father's will;
Or else the law of Athens yields you up—
Which by no means we may extenuate—   120
To death, or to a vow of single life.
Come, my Hippolyta. What cheer, my love?
Demetrius and Egeus, go along.
I must employ you in some business
Against° our nuptial, and confer with you   125
Of something nearly° that concerns yourselves.

Egeus. With duty and desire we follow you.
              Exeunt [all but Lysander and Hermia].

Lysander. How now, my love! Why is your cheek so
    pale?
How chance° the roses there do fade so fast?

Hermia. Belike° for want of rain, which I could well   130
    Beteem° them from the tempest of my eyes.

Lysander. Ay me! For aught that I could ever read,
    Could ever hear by tale or history,

106 *to his head* in his teeth   110 *spotted* i.e., morally stained
125 *Against* in preparation for   126 *nearly* closely   129 *How
chance* how does it come that   130 *Belike* perhaps   131 *Beteem*
bring forth

The course of true love never did run smooth;
135   But, either it was different in blood—

Hermia. O cross! Too high to be enthrallèd to low!

Lysander. Or else misgraffèd° in respect of years—

Hermia. O spite! Too old to be engaged to young!

Lysander. Or else it stood upon the choice of friends—

140   *Hermia.* O hell! To choose love by another's eyes!

Lysander. Or, if there were a sympathy in choice,
War, death, or sickness did lay siege to it,
Making it momentany° as a sound,
Swift as a shadow, short as any dream,
145   Brief as the lightning in the collied° night,
That, in a spleen,° unfolds both heaven and earth,
And ere a man hath power to say "Behold!"
The jaws of darkness do devour it up:
So quick bright things come to confusion.

150   *Hermia.* If then true lovers have been ever crossed,
It stands as an edict in destiny:
Then let us teach our trial patience,°
Because it is a customary cross,
As due to love as thoughts and dreams and sighs,
155   Wishes and tears, poor Fancy's° followers.

Lysander. A good persuasion.° Therefore, hear me,
    Hermia.
I have a widow aunt, a dowager
Of great revenue, and she hath no child.
From Athens is her house remote seven leagues,
160   And she respects me as her only son.
There, gentle Hermia, may I marry thee,
And to that place the sharp Athenian law
Cannot pursue us. If thou lovest me, then,

---

137 *misgraffèd* ill matched, misgrafted   143 *momentany* momentary, passing   145 *collied* blackened   146 *spleen* flash   152 *teach our trial patience* i.e., teach ourselves to be patient   155 *Fancy's* Love's   156 *persuasion* principle

Steal forth thy father's house tomorrow night;
And in the wood, a league without the town,   *165*
Where I did meet thee once with Helena,
To do observance to a morn of May,
There will I stay for thee.

Hermia.   My good Lysander!
I swear to thee, by Cupid's strongest bow,
By his best arrow with the golden head,°   *170*
By the simplicity of Venus' doves,
By that which knitteth souls and prospers loves,
And by that fire which burned the Carthage
    queen,°
When the false Troyan under sail was seen,
By all the vows that ever men have broke,   *175*
In number more than ever women spoke,
In that same place thou hast appointed me,
Tomorrow truly will I meet with thee.

Lysander. Keep promise, love. Look, here comes
    Helena.

Enter Helena.

Hermia. God speed fair Helena! Whither away?   *180*

Helena. Call you me fair? That fair again unsay.
Demetrius loves your fair.° O happy fair!
Your eyes are lodestars,° and your tongue's sweet
    air°
More tunable than lark to shepherd's ear,
When wheat is green, when hawthorn buds appear.   *185*
Sickness is catching. O, were favor° so,
Yours would I catch, fair Hermia, ere I go;
My ear should catch your voice, my eye your eye,

---

170 *arrow with the golden head* (Cupid's gold-headed arrows caused
love, the leaden ones dislike)   173 *Carthage queen* Dido (who
burned herself on a funeral pyre when the Trojan Aeneas left her)
182 *fair* beauty   183 *lodestars* guiding stars   183 *air* music
186 *favor* looks

My tongue should catch your tongue's sweet melody.
190 Were the world mine, Demetrius being bated,°
The rest I'd give to be to you translated.°
O, teach me how you look, and with what art
You sway the motion of Demetrius' heart!

Hermia. I frown upon him, yet he loves me still.

Helena. O that your frowns would teach my smiles
195   such skill!

Hermia. I give him curses, yet he gives me love.

Helena. O that my prayers could such affection move!

Hermia. The more I hate, the more he follows me.

Helena. The more I love, the more he hateth me.

200 *Hermia.* His folly, Helena, is no fault of mine.

Helena. None, but your beauty: would that fault were
mine!

Hermia. Take comfort. He no more shall see my face;
Lysander and myself will fly this place.
Before the time I did Lysander see,
205 Seemed Athens as a paradise to me.
O, then, what graces in my love do dwell,
That he hath turned a heaven unto a hell!

Lysander. Helen, to you our minds we will unfold.
Tomorrow night, when Phoebe° doth behold
210 Her silver visage in the wat'ry glass,
Decking with liquid pearl the bladed grass,
A time that lovers' flights doth still° conceal,
Through Athens' gates have we devised to steal.

Hermia. And in the wood, where often you and I
215 Upon faint primrose beds were wont to lie,
Emptying our bosoms of their counsel sweet,
There my Lysander and myself shall meet,

190 *bated* excepted   191 *translated* transformed   209 *Phoebe* the
moon   212 *still* always

And thence from Athens turn away our eyes,
To seek new friends and stranger companies.°
Farewell, sweet playfellow. Pray thou for us;   220
And good luck grant thee thy Demetrius!
Keep word, Lysander. We must starve our sight
From lovers' food till tomorrow deep midnight.

Lysander. I will, my Hermia.   *Exit Hermia.*
                    Helena, adieu.
As you on him, Demetrius dote on you!   225

                    Exit Lysander.

Helena. How happy some o'er other some° can be!
Through Athens I am thought as fair as she.
But what of that? Demetrius thinks not so;
He will not know what all but he do know.
And as he errs, doting on Hermia's eyes,   230
So I, admiring of his qualities.
Things base and vile, holding no quantity,°
Love can transpose to form and dignity.
Love looks not with the eyes, but with the mind,
And therefore is winged Cupid painted blind.   235
Nor hath Love's mind of any judgment taste;
Wings, and no eyes, figure° unheedy haste:
And therefore is Love said to be a child,
Because in choice he is so oft beguiled.
As waggish boys in game themselves forswear,   240
So the boy Love is perjured everywhere.
For ere Demetrius looked on Hermia's eyne,°
He hailed down oaths that he was only mine;
And when this hail some heat from Hermia felt,
So he dissolved, and show'rs of oaths did melt.   245
I will go tell him of fair Hermia's flight.
Then to the wood will he tomorrow night
Pursue her; and for this intelligence°

---

219 *stranger companies* the company of strangers   226 *some o'er other some* some in comparison with others   232 *holding no quantity* having no proportion (therefore unattractive)   237 *figure* symbolize   242 *eyne* eyes   248 *intelligence* piece of news

If I have thanks, it is a dear expense:°
250   But herein mean I to enrich my pain,
To have his sight thither and back again.   *Exit.*

[Scene II. *Quince's house.*]

*Enter Quince the Carpenter, and Snug the Joiner,
and Bottom the Weaver, and Flute the Bellows
Mender, and Snout the Tinker, and Starveling the
Tailor.°*

Quince. Is all our company here?

Bottom. You were best to call them generally,° man
by man, according to the scrip.

Quince. Here is the scroll of every man's name,
5   which is thought fit, through all Athens, to play in
our interlude° before the Duke and the Duchess,
on his wedding day at night.

Bottom. First, good Peter Quince, say what the play
treats on; then read the names of the actors; and
10   so grow to a point.

Quince. Marry,° our play is, "The most lamentable
comedy, and most cruel death of Pyramus and
Thisby."

Bottom. A very good piece of work, I assure you,

---

249 *dear expense* (1) expense gladly incurred (2) heavy cost (in
Demetrius' opinion)   I.ii.s.d. (the names of the clowns suggest their
trades. *Bottom* skein on which the yarn is wound; *Quince* quines,
blocks of wood used for building; *Snug* close-fitting; *Flute* suggesting
fluted bellows [for church organs]; *Snout* spout of a kettle;
Starveling an allusion to the proverbial thinness of tailors)   2 *generally* (Bottom means "individually")   6 *interlude* dramatic entertainment   11 *Marry* (an interjection, originally an oath, "By the
Virgin Mary")

and a merry. Now, good Peter Quince, call forth 15
your actors by the scroll. Masters, spread yourselves.

Quince. Answer as I call you. Nick Bottom, the
weaver.

Bottom. Ready. Name what part I am for, and pro- 20
ceed.

Quince. You, Nick Bottom, are set down for Pyramus.

Bottom. What is Pyramus? A lover, or a tyrant?

Quince. A lover that kills himself, most gallant, for
love. 25

Bottom. That will ask some tears in the true per-
forming of it: if I do it, let the audience look to
their eyes. I will move storms, I will condole° in
some measure. To the rest: yet my chief humor°
is for a tyrant. I could play Ercles° rarely, or a 30
part to tear a cat in, to make all split.

> The raging rocks
> And shivering shocks
> Shall break the locks
>   Of prison gates; 35
> And Phibbus' car°
> Shall shine from far,
> And make and mar
>   The foolish Fates.

This was lofty! Now name the rest of the players. 40
This is Ercles' vein, a tyrant's vein. A lover is
more condoling.

Quince. Francis Flute, the bellows mender.

Flute. Here, Peter Quince.

---

28 *condole* lament   29 *humor* disposition   30 *Ercles* Hercules (a
part notorious for ranting)   36 *Phibbus' car* (mispronunciation for
"Phoebus' car," or chariot, i.e., the sun)

45 *Quince.* Flute, you must take Thisby on you.

Flute. What is Thisby? A wand'ring knight?

Quince. It is the lady that Pyramus must love.

Flute. Nay, faith, let not me play a woman. I have
a beard coming.

50 *Quince.* That's all one.° You shall play it in a mask,
and you may speak as small° as you will.

Bottom. An° I may hide my face, let me play Thisby
too, I'll speak in a monstrous little voice, "Thisne,
Thisne!" "Ah Pyramus, my lover dear! Thy Thisby
55 dear, and lady dear!"

Quince. No, no; you must play Pyramus: and, Flute,
you Thisby.

Bottom. Well, proceed.

Quince. Robin Starveling, the tailor.

60 *Starveling.* Here, Peter Quince.

Quince. Robin Starveling, you must play Thisby's
mother. Tom Snout, the tinker.

Snout. Here, Peter Quince.

Quince. You, Pyramus' father: myself, Thisby's
65 father: Snug, the joiner; you, the lion's part. And
I hope here is a play fitted.

Snug. Have you the lion's part written? Pray you, if
it be, give it me, for I am slow of study.

Quince. You may do it extempore, for it is nothing
70 but roaring.

Bottom. Let me play the lion too. I will roar that° I
will do any man's heart good to hear me. I will
roar, that I will make the Duke say, "Let him roar
again, let him roar again."

50 *That's all one* it makes no difference   51 *small* softly   52 *An* if
71 *that* so that

Quince. An you should do it too terribly, you would 75
  fright the Duchess and the ladies, that they would
  shriek; and that were enough to hang us all.

All. That would hang us, every mother's son.

Bottom. I grant you, friends, if you should fright the
  ladies out of their wits, they would have no more 80
  discretion but to hang us: but I will aggravate°
  my voice so that I will roar you as gently as any
  sucking dove; I will roar you an 'twere° any nightingale.

Quince. You can play no part but Pyramus; for 85
  Pyramus is a sweet-faced man; a proper° man as
  one shall see in a summer's day; a most lovely,
  gentlemanlike man: therefore you must needs play
  Pyramus.

Bottom. Well, I will undertake it. What beard were 90
  I best to play it in?

Quince. Why, what you will.

Bottom. I will discharge it in either your straw-color
  beard, your orange-tawny beard, your purple-in-
  grain° beard, or your French-crown-color° beard, 95
  your perfit° yellow.

Quince. Some of your French crowns° have no hair
  at all, and then you will play barefaced.° But, masters, here are your parts; and I am to entreat you,
  request you, and desire you, to con° them by to- 100
  morrow night; and meet me in the palace wood, a
  mile without the town, by moonlight. There will
  we rehearse, for if we meet in the city, we shall be
  dogged with company, and our devices° known.

---

81 *aggravate* (Bottom means "moderate")   83 *an 'twere* as if it were
86 *proper* handsome   94–95 *purple-in-grain* dyed with a fast purple
95 *French-crown-color* color of French gold coin   96 *perfit* perfect
97 *crowns* (1) gold coins (2) heads bald from the French disease
(syphilis)   98 *barefaced* (1) bald (2) brazen   100 *con* study
104 *devices* plans

105 In the meantime I will draw a bill of properties,° such as our play wants. I pray you, fail me not.

Bottom. We will meet; and there we may rehearse most obscenely° and courageously. Take pains; be perfit: adieu.

110 *Quince.* At the Duke's Oak we meet.

Bottom. Enough; hold or cut bowstrings.°   *Exeunt.*

---

105 *bill of properties* list of stage furnishings   108 *obscenely* (Bottom means "seemly")   111 *hold or cut bowstrings* i.e., keep your word or give it up (?)

[ACT II

Scene I. *A wood near Athens.*]

*Enter a Fairy at one door, and Robin Goodfellow
[Puck] at another.*

Puck. How now, spirit! Whither wander you?

Fairy.   Over hill, over dale,
    Thorough bush, thorough brier,
Over park, over pale,°
    Thorough flood, thorough fire,   5
I do wander everywhere,
Swifter than the moon's sphere;°
And I serve the Fairy Queen,
To dew her orbs° upon the green.
The cowslips tall her pensioners° be: 10
In their gold coats spots you see;
Those be rubies, fairy favors,°
In those freckles live their savors.°
I must go seek some dewdrops here,
And hang a pearl in every cowslip's ear.   15

II.i.4 *pale* enclosed land, park   7 *moon's sphere* (according to the
Ptolemaic system the moon was fixed in a hollow sphere that sur-
rounded and revolved about the earth)   9 *orbs* fairy rings, i.e.,
circles of darker grass   10 *pensioners* bodyguards (referring to
Elizabeth I's bodyguard of fifty splendid young noblemen)
12 *favors* gifts   13 *savors* perfumes

Farewell, thou lob° of spirits; I'll be gone.
Our Queen and all her elves come here anon.

Puck. The King doth keep his revels here tonight.
Take heed the Queen come not within his sight.
20 For Oberon is passing fell and wrath,°
Because that she as her attendant hath
A lovely boy, stolen from an Indian king;
She never had so sweet a changeling.°
And jealous Oberon would have the child
25 Knight of his train, to trace° the forests wild.
But she perforce withholds the lovèd boy,
Crowns him with flowers, and makes him all her
    joy.
And now they never meet in grove or green,
By fountain clear, or spangled starlight sheen,°
30 But they do square,° that all their elves for fear
Creep into acorn cups and hide them there.

Fairy. Either I mistake your shape and making quite,
Or else you are that shrewd and knavish sprite
Called Robin Goodfellow. Are not you he
35 That frights the maidens of the villagery,°
Skim milk, and sometimes labor in the quern,°
And bootless° make the breathless housewife
    churn,
And sometime make the drink to bear no barm,°
Mislead night wanderers, laughing at their harm?
40 Those that Hobgoblin call you, and sweet Puck,
You do their work, and they shall have good luck.
Are not you he?

Puck.   Thou speakest aright;
I am that merry wanderer of the night.
I jest to Oberon, and make him smile,

---

16 *lob* lubber, clumsy fellow   20 *passing fell and wrath* very fierce
and angry   23 *changeling* (usually a child left behind by fairies in
exchange for one stolen, but here applied to the stolen child)   25
trace traverse   29 *starlight sheen* brightly shining starlight   30
square clash, quarrel   35 *villagery* villagers   36 *quern* hand mill for
grinding grain   37 *bootless* in vain   38 *barm* yeast, froth

When I a fat and bean-fed horse beguile,   45
Neighing in likeness of a filly foal:
And sometime lurk I in a gossip's° bowl,
In very likeness of a roasted crab;°
And when she drinks, against her lips I bob
And on her withered dewlap° pour the ale.   50
The wisest aunt, telling the saddest° tale,
Sometime for three-foot stool mistaketh me;
Then slip I from her bum, down topples she,
And "tailor"° cries, and falls into a cough;
And then the whole quire° hold their hips and
          laugh,   55
And waxen° in their mirth, and neeze,° and swear
A merrier hour was never wasted° there.
But, room, fairy! Here comes Oberon.

Fairy. And here my mistress. Would that he were
     gone!

*Enter [Oberon,] the King of Fairies, at one door,
with his train; and [Titania,] the Queen, at another,
with hers.*

Oberon. Ill met by moonlight, proud Titania.   60

Titania. What, jealous Oberon! Fairy, skip hence.
I have forsworn his bed and company.

Oberon. Tarry, rash wanton;° am not I thy lord?

Titania. Then I must be thy lady: but I know
When thou hast stolen away from fairy land   65
And in the shape of Corin° sat all day,
Playing on pipes of corn,° and versing love

---

47 *gossip's* old woman's 48 *crab* crab apple 50 *dewlap* fold of
skin on the throat 51 *saddest* most serious 54 *tailor* (suggesting
the posture of a tailor squatting; or a term of abuse: Middle English
taillard, "thief") 55 *quire* company, choir 56 *waxen* increase
56 *neeze* sneeze 57 *wasted* passed 63 *rash wanton* hasty willful creature 66 *Corin* (like *Phillida,* line 68, a traditional name for
a lover in pastoral poetry) 67 *pipes of corn* musical instruments
made of grain stalks

To amorous Phillida. Why art thou here,
Come from the farthest steep of India?
70 But that, forsooth, the bouncing° Amazon,
Your buskined° mistress and your warrior love,
To Theseus must be wedded, and you come
To give their bed joy and prosperity.

Oberon. How canst thou thus for shame, Titania,
75 Glance at my credit with Hippolyta,
Knowing I know thy love to Theseus?
Didst not thou lead him through the glimmering
night
From Perigenia, whom he ravishèd?
And make him with fair Aegles break his faith,
80 With Ariadne and Antiopa?°

Titania. These are the forgeries of jealousy:
And never, since the middle summer's spring,°
Met we on hill, in dale, forest, or mead,
By pavèd° fountain or by rushy brook,
85 Or in the beachèd margent° of the sea,
To dance our ringlets to the whistling wind,
But with thy brawls thou hast disturbed our sport.
Therefore the winds, piping to us in vain,
As in revenge, have sucked up from the sea
Contagious° fogs; which, falling in the land,
Hath every pelting° river made so proud,
That they have overborne their continents.°
The ox hath therefore stretched his yoke in vain,
The plowman lost his sweat, and the green corn°
Hath rotted ere his youth attained a beard;
The fold stands empty in the drownèd field,
And crows are fatted with the murrion flock;°

---

70 *bouncing* swaggering   71 *buskined* wearing a hunter's boot
(buskin)   78–80 *Perigenia, Aegles, Ariadne, Antiopa* (girls Theseus
loved and deserted)   82 *middle summer's spring* beginning of midsummer   84 *pavèd* i.e., with pebbly bottom   85 *margent* margin,
shore   90 *contagious* generating pestilence   91 *pelting* petty   92
continents containers (i.e., banks)   94 *corn* grain   97 *murrion
flock* flock dead of cattle disease (murrain)

The nine men's morris° is filled up with mud;
And the quaint mazes° in the wanton green,°
For lack of tread, are undistinguishable.   100
The human mortals want their winter here;
No night is now with hymn or carol blest.
Therefore the moon, the governess of floods,
Pale in her anger, washes all the air,
That rheumatic diseases do abound.   105
And thorough this distemperature° we see
The seasons alter: hoary-headed frosts
Fall in the fresh lap of the crimson rose,
And on old Hiems'° thin and icy crown
An odorous chaplet° of sweet summer buds   110
Is, as in mockery, set. The spring, the summer,
The childing° autumn, angry winter, change
Their wonted liveries;° and the mazèd° world,
By their increase, now knows not which is which.
And this same progeny of evils comes   115
From our debate,° from our dissension;
We are their parents and original.

Oberon. Do you amend it, then; it lies in you:
Why should Titania cross her Oberon?
I do but beg a little changeling boy,   120
To be my henchman.°

Titania.   Set your heart at rest.
The fairy land buys not° the child of me.
His mother was a vot'ress° of my order,
And, in the spicèd Indian air, by night,
Full often hath she gossiped by my side,   125
And sat with me on Neptune's yellow sands,

---

98 *nine men's morris* square cut in the turf (for a game in which
each player has nine counters or "men")   99 *quaint mazes* intricate
meandering paths on the grass (kept fresh by running along them)
99 *wanton green* grass growing without check   106 *distemperature*
disturbance in nature   109 *old Hiems'* the winter's   110 *chaplet*
wreath   112 *childing* breeding, fruitful   113 *wonted liveries* accus-
tomed apparel   113 *mazèd* bewildered   116 *debate* quarrel   121
henchman page   122 *The fairy land buys not* i.e., even your whole
domain could not buy   123 *vot'ress* woman who has taken a vow

Marking th' embarkèd traders on the flood;
When we have laughed to see the sails conceive
And grow big-bellied with the wanton wind;
130 Which she, with pretty and with swimming gait
Following—her womb then rich with my young
        squire—
Would imitate, and sail upon the land,
To fetch me trifles, and return again,
As from a voyage, rich with merchandise.
135 But she, being mortal, of that boy did die;
And for her sake do I rear up her boy,
And for her sake I will not part with him.

Oberon. How long within this wood intend you stay?

Titania. Perchance till after Theseus' wedding day.
140 If you will patiently dance in our round,°
And see our moonlight revels, go with us.
If not, shun me, and I will spare° your haunts.

Oberon. Give me that boy, and I will go with thee.

Titania. Not for thy fairy kingdom. Fairies, away!
145 We shall chide downright, if I longer stay.
                    Exeunt [*Titania with her train*].

Oberon. Well, go thy way. Thou shalt not from this
        grove
Till I torment thee for this injury.
My gentle Puck, come hither. Thou rememb'rest
Since° once I sat upon a promontory,
150 And heard a mermaid, on a dolphin's back,
Uttering such dulcet and harmonious breath,
That the rude sea grew civil° at her song,
And certain stars shot madly from their spheres,
To hear the sea maid's music.

Puck.   I remember.

155 *Oberon.* That very time I saw, but thou couldst not,
Flying between the cold moon and the earth,

140 *round* circular dance   142 *spare* keep away from   149 *Since*
when   152 *civil* well behaved

Cupid all armed. A certain aim he took
At a fair vestal° thronèd by the west,
And loosed his love shaft smartly from his bow,
As it should° pierce a hundred thousand hearts.   160
But I might° see young Cupid's fiery shaft
Quenched in the chaste beams of the wat'ry moon,
And the imperial vot'ress passèd on,
In maiden meditation, fancy-free.°
Yet marked I where the bolt of Cupid fell.   165
It fell upon a little western flower,
Before milk-white, now purple with love's wound,
And maidens call it love-in-idleness.°
Fetch me that flow'r; the herb I showed thee once:
The juice of it on sleeping eyelids laid   170
Will make or man or woman° madly dote
Upon the next live creature that it sees.
Fetch me this herb, and be thou here again
Ere the leviathan° can swim a league.

Puck. I'll put a girdle round about the earth   175
In forty minutes.   [*Exit.*]

Oberon.   Having once this juice,
I'll watch Titania when she is asleep,
And drop the liquor of it in her eyes.
The next thing then she waking looks upon,
Be it on lion, bear, or wolf, or bull,   180
On meddling monkey, or on busy° ape,
She shall pursue it with the soul of love.
And ere I take this charm from off her sight,
As I can take it with another herb,
I'll make her render up her page to me.   185
But who comes here? I am invisible,
And I will overhear their conference.

Enter Demetrius, Helena following him.

---

158 *vestal* virgin (possibly an allusion to Elizabeth, the Virgin
Queen)   160 *As it should* as if it would   161 *might* could   164
fancy-free free from the power of love   168 *love-in-idleness* pansy
171 *or man or woman* either man or woman   174 *leviathan* sea
monster, whale   181 *busy* meddlesome

Demetrius. I love thee not, therefore pursue me not.
Where is Lysander and fair Hermia?
190 The one I'll slay, the other slayeth me.
Thou told'st me they were stol'n unto this wood;
And here am I, and wood° within this wood,
Because I cannot meet my Hermia.
Hence, get thee gone, and follow me no more!

195 *Helena.* You draw me, you hardhearted adamant;°
But yet you draw not iron, for my heart
Is true as steel. Leave you your power to draw,
And I shall have no power to follow you.

Demetrius. Do I entice you? Do I speak you fair?°
200 Or, rather, do I not in plainest truth
Tell you, I do not nor I cannot love you?

Helena. And even for that do I love you the more.
I am your spaniel; and, Demetrius,
The more you beat me, I will fawn on you.
205 Use me but as your spaniel, spurn me, strike me,
Neglect me, lose me; only give me leave,
Unworthy as I am, to follow you.
What worser place can I beg in your love—
And yet a place of high respect with me—
210 Than to be usèd as you use your dog?

Demetrius. Tempt not too much the hatred of my
      spirit,
For I am sick when I do look on thee.

Helena. And I am sick when I look not on you.

Demetrius. You do impeach° your modesty too much,
215 To leave the city, and commit yourself
Into the hands of one that loves you not,
To trust the opportunity of night
And the ill counsel of a desert° place
With the rich worth of your virginity.

192 *wood* out of my mind (with perhaps an additional pun on
"wooed")   195 *adamant* (1) very hard gem (2) loadstone, magnet
199 *speak you fair* speak kindly to you   214 *impeach* expose to
reproach   218 *desert* deserted, uninhabited

Helena. Your virtue is my privilege.° For that   220
  It is not night when I do see your face,
  Therefore I think I am not in the night;
  Nor doth this wood lack worlds of company,
  For you in my respect° are all the world.
  Then how can it be said I am alone,   225
  When all the world is here to look on me?

Demetrius. I'll run from thee and hide me in the
      brakes,°
  And leave thee to the mercy of wild beasts.

Helena. The wildest hath not such a heart as you.
  Run when you will, the story shall be changed: 230
  Apollo flies, and Daphne° holds the chase;
  The dove pursues the griffin;° the mild hind°
  Makes speed to catch the tiger; bootless speed,
  When cowardice pursues, and valor flies.

Demetrius. I will not stay° thy questions. Let me go!   235
  Or, if thou follow me, do not believe
  But I shall do thee mischief in the wood.

Helena. Ay, in the temple, in the town, the field,
  You do me mischief. Fie, Demetrius!
  Your wrongs do set a scandal on my sex.   240
  We cannot fight for love, as men may do;
  We should be wooed, and were not made to woo.
                              [*Exit Demetrius.*]
  I'll follow thee, and make a heaven of hell,
  To die upon° the hand I love so well.   .   [*Exit.*]

Oberon. Fare thee well, nymph: ere he do leave this
      grove,   245
  Thou shalt fly him, and he shall seek thy love.

---

220 *Your virtue is my privilege* your inherent power is my warrant
224 *in my respect* in my opinion   227 *brakes* thickets   231 *Daphne*
a nymph who fled from Apollo (at her prayer she was changed into
a laurel tree)   232 *griffin* fabulous monster with an eagle's head
and a lion's body   232 *hind* doe   235 *stay* wait for   244 *To die
upon* dying by

Enter Puck.

Hast thou the flower there? Welcome, wanderer.

Puck. Ay, there it is.

Oberon.   I pray thee, give it me.
I know a bank where the wild thyme blows,
250   Where oxlips and the nodding violet grows,
Quite overcanopied with luscious woodbine,
With sweet musk roses, and with eglantine.
There sleeps Titania sometime of the night,
Lulled in these flowers with dances and delight;
255   And there the snake throws° her enameled skin,
Weed° wide enough to wrap a fairy in.
And with the juice of this I'll streak her eyes,
And make her full of hateful fantasies.
Take thou some of it, and seek through this grove.
260   A sweet Athenian lady is in love
With a disdainful youth. Anoint his eyes;
But do it when the next thing he espies
May be the lady. Thou shalt know the man
By the Athenian garments he hath on.
265   Effect it with some care that he may prove
More fond on her° than she upon her love:
And look thou meet me ere the first cock crow.

Puck. Fear not, my lord, your servant shall do so.
                                        Exeunt.

[Scene II.   *Another part of the wood*.]

Enter Titania, Queen of Fairies, with her train.

Titania. Come, now a roundel° and a fairy song;
Then, for the third part of a minute, hence;

255 *throws* casts off   256 *Weed* garment   266 *fond on her* foolishly
in love with her   II.ii.1 *roundel* dance in a ring

Some to kill cankers in the musk-rose buds,
Some war with reremice° for their leathern wings
To make my small elves coats, and some keep back   5
The clamorous owl, that nightly hoots and wonders
At our quaint° spirits. Sing me now asleep.
Then to your offices, and let me rest.

Fairies sing.

1st   You spotted snakes with double tongue,
Fairy.   Thorny hedgehogs, be not seen;   10
            Newts and blindworms,° do no wrong,
                Come not near our Fairy Queen.

Chorus.   Philomele,° with melody
                Sing in our sweet lullaby;
            Lulla, lulla, lullaby, lulla, lulla, lullaby: 15
                Never harm
                Nor spell nor charm,
            Come our lovely lady nigh;
            So, good night, with lullaby.

1st   Weaving spiders, come not here;   20
Fairy.   Hence, you long-legged spinners, hence!
            Beetles black, approach not near;
                Worm nor snail, do no offense.

Chorus.   Philomele, with melody, &c.

2nd   Hence, away! Now all is well.   25
Fairy.   One aloof stand sentinel.
                    [*Exeunt Fairies. Titania sleeps.*]

*Enter Oberon [and squeezes the flower on
        Titania's eyelids].*

Oberon.   What thou seest when thou dost wake,
            Do it for thy truelove take;
            Love and languish for his sake.
            Be it ounce,° or cat, or bear,   30

4 *reremice* bats   7 *quaint* dainty   11 *blindworms* small snakes
13 *Philomele* nightingale   30 *ounce* lynx

   Pard,° or boar with bristled hair,
   In thy eye that shall appear
   When thou wak'st, it is thy dear.
   Wake when some vile thing is near. [*Exit.*]

   Enter Lysander and Hermia.

35 *Lysander.* Fair love, you faint with wand'ring in the
  wood;
  And to speak troth,° I have forgot our way.
  We'll rest us, Hermia, if you think it good,
  And tarry for the comfort of the day.

Hermia. Be't so, Lysander. Find you out a bed;
40 For I upon this bank will rest my head.

Lysander. One turf shall serve as pillow for us both,
  One heart, one bed, two bosoms, and one troth.

Hermia. Nay, good Lysander. For my sake, my dear,
  Lie further off yet, do not lie so near.

45 *Lysander.* O, take the sense,° sweet, of my innocence!
  Love takes the meaning° in love's conference.
  I mean, that my heart unto yours is knit,
  So that but one heart we can make of it:
  Two bosoms interchainèd with an oath;
50 So then two bosoms and a single troth.°
  Then by your side no bed-room me deny,
  For lying so, Hermia, I do not lie.°

Hermia. Lysander riddles very prettily.
  Now much beshrew° my manners and my pride,
55 If Hermia meant to say Lysander lied.
  But, gentle friend, for love and courtesy
  Lie further off, in human modesty.
  Such separation as may well be said

31 *Pard* leopard 36 *troth* truth 45 *take the sense* understand the
true meaning 46 *Love takes the meaning* lovers understand the
true meaning of what they say to each other 50 *troth* faithful love
52 *lie* be untrue 54 *beshrew* curse (but commonly, as here, in a
light sense)

Becomes a virtuous bachelor and a maid,
So far be distant; and, good night, sweet friend. *60*
Thy love ne'er alter till thy sweet life end!

Lysander. Amen, amen, to that fair prayer, say I,
And then end life when I end loyalty!
Here is my bed. Sleep give thee all his rest!

Hermia. With half that wish the wisher's eyes be
pressed!   [*They sleep.*] *65*

Enter Puck.

Puck. Through the forest have I gone,
But Athenian found I none,
On whose eyes I might approve°
This flower's force in stirring love.
Night and silence.—Who is here? *70*
Weeds° of Athens he doth wear:
This is he, my master said,
Despisèd the Athenian maid;
And here the maiden, sleeping sound,
On the dank and dirty ground. *75*
Pretty soul! She durst not lie
Near this lack-love, this kill-courtesy.
Churl,° upon thy eyes I throw
All the power this charm doth owe.°
When thou wak'st, let love forbid *80*
Sleep his seat on thy eyelid.
So awake when I am gone,
For I must now to Oberon.   *Exit.*

Enter Demetrius and Helena, running.

Helena. Stay, though thou kill me, sweet Demetrius.

Demetrius. I charge thee, hence, and do not haunt me
thus. *85*

---

68 *approve* try   71 *Weeds* garments   78 *Churl* boorish   fellow
79 *owe* possess

Helena. O, wilt thou darkling° leave me? Do not so.

Demetrius. Stay, on thy peril! I alone will go. [*Exit.*]

Helena. O, I am out of breath in this fond° chase!
The more my prayer, the lesser is my grace.
90 Happy is Hermia, wheresoe'er she lies,
For she hath blessèd and attractive eyes.
How came her eyes so bright? Not with salt tears.
If so, my eyes are oft'ner washed than hers.
No, no, I am as ugly as a bear,
95 For beasts that meet me run away for fear.
Therefore no marvel though Demetrius
Do, as a monster, fly my presence thus.
What wicked and dissembling glass of mine
Made me compare with Hermia's sphery eyne?°
100 But who is here? Lysander! On the ground!
Dead? Or asleep? I see no blood, no wound.
Lysander, if you live, good sir, awake.

Lysander. [*Awaking*] And run through fire I will for
thy sweet sake.
Transparent° Helena! Nature shows art,
105 That through thy bosom makes me see thy heart.
Where is Demetrius? O, how fit a word
Is that vile name to perish on my sword!

Helena. Do not say so, Lysander, say not so.
What though he love your Hermia? Lord, what
though?
110 Yet Hermia still loves you. Then be content.

Lysander. Content with Hermia! No; I do repent
The tedious minutes I with her have spent.
Not Hermia but Helena I love:
Who will not change a raven for a dove?
115 The will° of man is by his reason swayed
And reason says you are the worthier maid.
Things growing are not ripe until their season:
So I, being young, till now ripe not° to reason.

86 *darkling* in the dark   88 *fond* (1) doting (2) foolish   99 *sphery
eyne* starry eyes   104 *Transparent* bright   115 *will* desire   118 *ripe
not* have not ripened

And touching now the point of human skill,°   120
Reason becomes the marshal to my will,
And leads me to your eyes, where I o'erlook
Love's stories, written in love's richest book.

Helena. Wherefore was I to this keen mockery born?
When at your hands did I deserve this scorn?
Is't not enough, is't not enough, young man,   125
That I did never, no, nor never can,
Deserve a sweet look from Demetrius' eye,
But you must flout° my insufficiency?
Good troth,° you do me wrong, good sooth, you do,
In such disdainful manner me to woo.   130
But fare you well. Perforce I must confess
I thought you lord of more true gentleness.°
O, that a lady, of one man refused,
Should of another therefore be abused!   *Exit.*

Lysander. She sees not Hermia. Hermia, sleep thou
    there,   135
And never mayst thou come Lysander near!
For as a surfeit of the sweetest things
The deepest loathing to the stomach brings,
Or as the heresies that men do leave
Are hated most of those they did deceive,   140
So thou, my surfeit and my heresy,
Of all be hated, but the most of me!
And, all my powers, address° your love and might
To honor Helen and to be her knight!   *Exit.*

Hermia. [*Awaking*] Help me, Lysander, help me! Do
    thy best   145
To pluck this crawling serpent from my breast!
Ay me, for pity! What a dream was here!
Lysander, look how I do quake with fear.
Methought a serpent eat° my heart away,

119 *touching now . . . human skill* now reaching the fulness of human
reason   128 *flout* jeer at   129 *Good troth* indeed (an expletive, like
"good sooth")   132 *gentleness* noble character   143 *address* apply
149 *eat* ate (pronounced "et")

150 And you sat smiling at his cruel prey.°
Lysander! What, removed? Lysander! Lord!
What, out of hearing? Gone? No sound, no word?
Alack, where are you? Speak, an if° you hear;
Speak, of° all loves! I swoon almost with fear.
155 No? Then I well perceive you are not nigh.
Either death or you I'll find immediately.   *Exit.*

150 *prey* act of preying   153 *an if* if   154 *of* for the sake of

[ACT III

Scene I. *The wood. Titania lying asleep.*]

Enter the clowns: [*Quince, Snug, Bottom, Flute,*
Snout, and Starveling].

Bottom. Are we all met?

Quince. Pat,° pat; and here's a marvail's° convenient
place for our rehearsal. This green plot shall be
our stage, this hawthorn brake° our tiring house,°
and we will do it in action as we will do it before   5
the Duke.

Bottom. Peter Quince?

Quince. What sayest thou, bully° Bottom?

Bottom. There are things in this comedy of Pyramus
and Thisby that will never please. First, Pyramus   10
must draw a sword to kill himself; which the ladies
cannot abide. How answer you that?

Snout. By'r lakin,° a parlous° fear.

Starveling. I believe we must leave the killing out,
when all is done.   15

III.i.2 *Pat* exactly, on the dot   2 *marvail's* (Quince means "marvelous")   4 *brake* thicket   4 *tiring house* attiring house, dressing
room   8 *bully* good fellow   13 *By'r lakin* by our lady (ladykin =
little lady)   13 *parlous* perilous, terrible

71

Bottom. Not a whit. I have a device to make all well.
Write me a prologue, and let the prologue seem to
say, we will do no harm with our swords, and that
Pyramus is not killed indeed; and, for the more
20   better assurance, tell them that I Pyramus am not
Pyramus, but Bottom the weaver. This will put
them out of fear.

Quince. Well, we will have such a prologue, and it
shall be written in eight and six.°

25   *Bottom.* No, make it two more; let it be written in
eight and eight.

Snout. Will not the ladies be afeared of the lion?

Starveling. I fear it, I promise you.

Bottom. Masters, you ought to consider with your-
30   selves. To bring in—God shield us!—a lion among
ladies, is a most dreadful thing. For there is not a
more fearful wild fowl than your lion living; and
we ought to look to't.

Snout. Therefore another prologue must tell he is not
35   a lion.

Bottom. Nay, you must name his name, and half his
face must be seen through the lion's neck, and he
himself must speak through, saying thus, or to the
same defect—"Ladies"—or, "Fair ladies—I would
40   wish you"—or, "I would request you"—or, "I
would entreat you—not to fear, not to tremble: my
life for yours. If you think I come hither as a lion,
it were pity of my life.° No, I am no such thing.
I am a man as other men are." And there indeed
45   let him name his name, and tell them plainly, he is
Snug the joiner.

Quince. Well, it shall be so. But there is two hard
things; that is, to bring the moonlight into a

---

24 *in eight and six* in alternate lines of eight and six syllables (ballad
stanza)   43 *pity of my life* a bad thing for me

chamber; for, you know, Pyramus and Thisby
meet by moonlight.   50

Snout. Doth the moon shine that night we play our
play?

Bottom. A calendar, a calendar! Look in the almanac;
find out moonshine, find out moonshine.

Quince. Yes, it doth shine that night.   55

Bottom. Why, then may you leave a casement of the
great chamber window, where we play, open, and
the moon may shine in at the casement.

Quince. Ay; or else one must come in with a bush of
thorns° and a lantern, and say he comes to dis-   60
figure,° or to present, the person of Moonshine.
Then, there is another thing: we must have a wall
in the great chamber; for Pyramus and Thisby,
says the story, did talk through the chink of a
wall.   65

Snout. You can never bring in a wall. What say you,
Bottom?

Bottom. Some man or other must present Wall: and
let him have some plaster, or some loam, or some
roughcast° about him, to signify Wall; and let him   70
hold his fingers thus, and through that cranny shall
Pyramus and Thisby whisper.

Quince. If that may be, then all is well. Come, sit
down, every mother's son, and rehearse your parts.
Pyramus, you begin. When you have spoken your   75
speech, enter into that brake; and so everyone according to his cue.

Enter Robin [Puck].

59–60 *bush of thorns* (legend held that the man in the moon had
been placed there for gathering firewood on Sunday)   60-61 *disfigure* (Bottom means "figure," "represent")   70 *roughcast* lime
mixed with gravel to plaster outside walls

Puck. What hempen homespuns° have we swagg'ring
    here,
    So near the cradle of the Fairy Queen?
80   What, a play toward!° I'll be an auditor;
    An actor too perhaps, if I see cause.

Quince. Speak, Pyramus. Thisby, stand forth.

Pyramus [*Bottom*]. Thisby, the flowers of odious
    savors sweet—

Quince. Odors, odors.

85 *Pyramus.* —odors savors sweet:
    So hath thy breath, my dearest Thisby dear.
    But hark, a voice! Stay thou but here awhile,
    And by and by° I will to thee appear.   *Exit.*

Puck. A stranger Pyramus than e'er played here!
                             [*Exit.*]

90 *Thisby* [*Flute*]. Must I speak now?

Quince. Ay, marry, must you. For you must under-
    stand he goes but to see a noise that he heard, and
    is to come again.

Thisby. Most radiant Pyramus, most lily-white of hue,
95   Of color like the red rose on triumphant brier,
    Most brisky juvenal,° and eke° most lovely Jew,
    As true as truest horse, that yet would never tire,
    I'll meet thee, Pyramus, at Ninny's° tomb.

Quince. "Ninus' tomb," man. Why, you must not
100   speak that yet. That you answer to Pyramus. You
    speak all your part at once, cues and all. Pyramus
    enter. Your cue is past; it is "never tire."

Thisby. O—as true as truest horse, that yet would
    never tire.

---

78 *hempen homespuns* coarse follows (clad in homespun cloth of
hemp)   80 *toward* in preparation   88 *by and by* shortly   96 *ju-*
venal youth   96 *eke* also   98 *Ninny's* (blunder for "Ninus'";
Ninus was the legendary founder of Nineveh)

[*Re-enter Puck, and Bottom with an ass's head.*]

Pyramus. If I were fair, Thisby, I were only thine.

Quince. O monstrous! O strange! We are haunted. 105
  Pray, masters! Fly, masters! Help!
            [*Exeunt all the clowns but Bottom.*]

Puck. I'll follow you, I'll lead you about a round,°
    Through bog, through bush, through brake,
        through brier.
  Sometime a horse I'll be, sometime a hound,
    A hog, a headless bear, sometime a fire;   110
  And neigh, and bark, and grunt, and roar, and
        burn,
  Like horse, hound, hog, bear, fire, at every turn.
                                        Exit.

Bottom. Why do they run away? This is a knavery of
  them to make me afeard.

                  Enter Snout.

Snout. O Bottom, thou art changed! What do I see 115
  on thee?

Bottom. What do you see? You see an ass head of
  your own, do you?   [*Exit Snout.*]

                  Enter Quince.

Quince. Bless thee, Bottom! Bless thee! Thou art
  translated.°   *Exit.* 120

Bottom. I see their knavery. This is to make an ass
  of me; to fright me, if they could. But I will not
  stir from this place, do what they can. I will walk
  up and down here, and will sing, that they shall
  hear I am not afraid.   [*Sings.*] 125

107 *about a round* roundabout   120 *translated* transformed

      The woosel° cock so black of hue,
        With orange-tawny bill,
      The throstle with his note so true,
        The wren with little quill°—

Titania. [*Awaking*] What angel wakes me from my
130   flow'ry bed?

Bottom. [*Sings*] The finch, the sparrow, and the lark,
        The plain-song cuckoo° gray,
          Whose note full many a man doth
            mark,
          And dares not answer nay—
135   for, indeed, who would set his wit° to so foolish
    a bird? Who would give a bird the lie,° though he
    cry "cuckoo" never so?°

Titania. I pray thee, gentle mortal, sing again:
    Mine ear is much enamored of thy note;
140   So is mine eye enthrallèd to thy shape;
    And thy fair virtue's force perforce doth move me
    On the first view to say, to swear, I love thee.

Bottom. Methinks, mistress, you should have little
    reason for that. And yet, to say the truth, reason
145   and love keep little company together nowadays;
    the more the pity, that some honest neighbors will
    not make them friends. Nay, I can gleek° upon
    occasion.

Titania. Thou art as wise as thou art beautiful.

150 *Bottom.* Not so, neither; but if I had wit enough to
    get out of this wood, I have enough to serve mine
    own turn.

Titania. Out of this wood do not desire to go.

---

126 *woosel* ouzel, blackbird   129 *quill* (literally, "reed pipe"; here, "piping voice")   132 *the plain-song cuckoo* the cuckoo, who sings a simple song   135 *set his wit* use his intelligence to answer   136 *give a bird the lie* contradict a bird (the cuckoo's song supposedly tells a man he is a cuckold)   137 *never so* ever so often   147 *gleek* make a satirical jest

Thou shalt remain here, whether thou wilt or no.
I am a spirit of no common rate.°   155
The summer still doth tend° upon my state;
And I do love thee. Therefore, go with me.
I'll give thee fairies to attend on thee,
And they shall fetch thee jewels from the deep,
And sing, while thou on pressèd flowers dost sleep: 160
And I will purge thy mortal grossness so,
That thou shalt like an airy spirit go.
Peaseblossom! Cobweb! Moth!° And Mustardseed!

Enter four Fairies
[Peaseblossom, Cobweb, Moth, and Mustardseed].

Peaseblossom. Ready.

Cobweb.   And I.

Moth.   And I.

Mustardseed.   And I.

All.   Where shall we go.

Titania. Be kind and courteous to this gentleman;   165
   Hop in his walks, and gambol in his eyes;
   Feed him with apricocks and dewberries,°
   With purple grapes, green figs, and mulberries;
   The honey bags steal from the humblebees,°
   And for night tapers crop their waxen thighs,   170
   And light them at the fiery glowworm's eyes,
   To have my love to bed and to arise;
   And pluck the wings from painted butterflies,
   To fan the moonbeams from his sleeping eyes.
   Nod to him, elves, and do him courtesies.   175

Peaseblossom. Hail, mortal!

Cobweb.   Hail!

---

155 *rate* rank   156 *still doth tend* always waits upon   163 *Moth*
(pronounced "mote," and probably a speck rather than an insect is
denoted)   167 *apricocks and dewberries* apricots and blackberries
169 *humblebees* bumblebees

Moth. Hail!

Mustardseed. Hail!

Bottom. I cry your worships mercy,° heartily: I beseech your worship's name.

Cobweb. Cobweb.

180 *Bottom.* I shall desire you of more acquaintance,° good Master Cobweb: if I cut my finger,° I shall make bold with you. Your name, honest gentleman?

Peaseblossom. Peaseblossom.

185 *Bottom.* I pray you, commend me to Mistress Squash,° your mother, and to Master Peascod, your father. Good Master Peaseblossom. I shall desire you of more acquaintance too. Your name, I beseech you, sir?

190 *Mustardseed.* Mustardseed.

Bottom. Good Master Mustardseed, I know your patience well. That same cowardly, giantlike ox-beef hath devoured° many a gentleman of your house. I promise you your kindred hath made my eyes 195 water ere now. I desire you of more acquaintance, good Master Mustardseed.

Titania. Come, wait upon him; lead him to my bower.
  The moon methinks looks with a wat'ry eye;
  And when she weeps, weeps every little flower,
200 Lamenting some enforcèd° chastity.
  Tie up my lover's tongue, bring him silently.
        Exit [Titania with Bottom and Fairies].

---

177 *I cry your worships mercy* I beg pardon of your honors   180 *I shall desire you of more acquaintance* I shall want to be better acquainted with you   181 *if I cut my finger* (cobweb was used for stanching blood)   185 *Squash* unripe pea pod   193 *devoured* (because beef is often eaten with mustard)   200 *enforcèd* violated

[Scene II.   *Another part of the wood.*]

Enter [Oberon,] King of Fairies, and Robin
Goodfellow [Puck].

Oberon. I wonder if Titania be awaked;
 Then, what it was that next came in her eye,
 Which she must dote on in extremity.°
 Here comes my messenger. How now, mad spirit!
 What night-rule° now about this haunted grove? 5

Puck. My mistress with a monster is in love.
 Near to her close° and consecrated bower,
 While she was in her dull and sleeping hour,
 A crew of patches,° rude mechanicals,°
 That work for bread upon Athenian stalls, 10
 Were met together to rehearse a play,
 Intended for great Theseus' nuptial day.
 The shallowest thickskin of that barren sort,°
 Who Pyramus presented in their sport,
 Forsook his scene, and entered in a brake. 15
 When I did him at this advantage take,
 An ass's nole° I fixèd on his head.
 Anon° his Thisby must be answerèd,
 And forth my mimic comes. When they him spy,
 As wild geese that the creeping fowler eye, 20
 Or russet-pated choughs, many in sort,°
 Rising and cawing at the gun's report,
 Sever themselves and madly sweep the sky,
 So, at his sight, away his fellows fly;

III.ii.3 *in extremity* to the extreme 5 *night-rule* happenings during
the night 7 *close* private, secret 9 *patches* fools, clowns 9 *rude
mechanicals* uneducated workingmen 13 *barren sort* stupid group
17 *nole* "noodle," head 18 *Anon* presently 21 *russet-pated . . . in
sort* gray-headed jackdaws, many in a flock

25 And, at our stamp, here o'er and o'er one falls;
He murder cries, and help from Athens calls.
Their sense thus weak, lost with their fears thus
    strong,
Made senseless things begin to do them wrong;
For briers and thorns at their apparel snatch;
30 Some sleeves, some hats, from yielders all things
    catch.
I led them on in this distracted fear,
And left sweet Pyramus translated there:
When in that moment, so it came to pass,
Titania waked, and straightway loved an ass.

35 *Oberon.* This falls out better than I could devise.
But hast thou yet latched° the Athenian's eyes
With the love juice, as I did bid thee do?

Puck. I took him sleeping—that is finished too—
And the Athenian woman by his side;
40 That, when he waked, of force° she must be eyed.

Enter Demetrius and Hermia.

Oberon. Stand close:° this is the same Athenian.

Puck. This is the woman, but not this the man.

Demetrius. O, why rebuke you him that loves you so?
Lay breath so bitter on your bitter foe.

45 *Hermia.* Now I but chide; but I should use thee worse,
For thou, I fear, hast given me cause to curse.
If thou hast slain Lysander in his sleep,
Being o'er shoes in blood, plunge in the deep,
And kill me too.
50 The sun was not so true unto the day
As he to me. Would he have stolen away
From sleeping Hermia? I'll believe as soon
This whole° earth may be bored, and that the moon
May through the center creep, and so displease

36 *latched* fastened (or possibly "moistened")   40 *of force* by
necessity   41 *close* concealed   53 *whole* solid

Her brother's° noontide with th' Antipodes.   55
It cannot be but thou hast murd'red him.
So should a murderer look, so dead,° so grim.

Demetrius. So should the murdered look; and so
   should I,
Pierced through the heart with your stern cruelty.
Yet you, the murderer, look as bright, as clear,   60
As yonder Venus in her glimmering sphere.

Hermia. What's this to my Lysander? Where is he?
Ah, good Demetrius, wilt thou give him me?

Demetrius. I had rather give his carcass to my hounds.

Hermia. Out, dog! Out, cur! Thou driv'st me past the
   bounds   65
Of maiden's patience. Hast thou slain him, then?
Henceforth be never numb'red among men!
O, once tell true! Tell true, even for my sake!
Durst thou have looked upon him being awake?
And hast thou killed him sleeping? O brave touch!°   70
Could not a worm, an adder, do so much?
An adder did it; for with doubler tongue
Than thine, thou serpent, never adder stung.

Demetrius. You spend your passion on a misprised
   mood:°
I am not guilty of Lysander's blood;   75
Nor is he dead, for aught that I can tell.

Hermia. I pray thee, tell me then that he is well.

Demetrius. An if I could, what should I get therefore?°

Hermia. A privilege, never to see me more.
And from thy hated presence part I so.
See me no more, whether he be dead or no.   *Exit*.   80

Demetrius. There is no following her in this fierce vein.

55 *Her brother's* i.e., the sun's   57 *dead* deadly pale   70 *brave touch* splendid exploit (ironic)   74 *misprised mood* mistaken anger 78 *therefore* in return

Here therefore for a while I will remain.
So sorrow's heaviness doth heavier grow
85 For debt that bankrout sleep doth sorrow owe;°
Which now in some slight measure it will pay,
If for his tender° here I make some stay.

Lie down [*and sleep*].

Oberon. What hast thou done? Thou hast mistaken quite,
And laid the love juice on some truelove's sight.
90 Of thy misprision° must perforce ensue
Some true love turned, and not a false turned true.

Puck. Then fate o'errules, that, one man holding troth,
A million fail, confounding oath on oath.°

Oberon. About the wood go swifter than the wind,
95 And Helena of Athens look thou find.
All fancy-sick° she is and pale of cheer,°
With sighs of love, that costs the fresh blood dear:
By some illusion see thou bring her here.
I'll charm his eyes against she do appear.°

100 *Puck.* I go, I go; look how I go,
Swifter than arrow from the Tartar's bow.   [*Exit.*]

Oberon. Flower of this purple dye,
Hit with Cupid's archery,
Sink in apple of his eye.
105 When his love he doth espy,
Let her shine as gloriously
As the Venus of the sky.
When thou wak'st, if she be by,
Beg of her for remedy.

Enter Puck.

---

85 *For debt . . . sorrow owe* because of the debt that bankrupt sleep owes to sorrow   87 *tender* offer   90 *misprision* mistake   93 *confounding oath on oath* breaking oath after oath   96 *fancy-sick* lovesick   96 *cheer* face   99 *against she do appear* in preparation for her appearance

Puck. Captain of our fairy band,   *110*
   Helena is here at hand;
   And the youth, mistook by me,
   Pleading for a lover's fee.
   Shall we their fond pageant° see?
   Lord, what fools these mortals be!   *115*

Oberon. Stand aside. The noise they make
   Will cause Demetrius to awake.

Puck. Then will two at once woo one;
   That must needs be sport alone;°
   And those things do best please me   *120*
   That befall prepost'rously.

Enter Lysander and Helena.

Lysander. Why should you think that I should woo in
      scorn?
   Scorn and derision never come in tears:
   Look, when I vow, I weep; and vows so born,
      In their nativity all truth appears.   *125*
   How can these things in me seem scorn to you,
   Bearing the badge of faith,° to prove them true?

Helena. You do advance° your cunning more and
      more.
   When truth kills truth, O devilish-holy fray!
   These vows are Hermia's: will you give her o'er? *130*
      Weigh oath with oath, and you will nothing
         weigh.
   Your vows to her and me, put in two scales,
   Will even weigh; and both as light as tales.

Lysander. I had no judgment when to her I swore.

Helena. Nor none, in my mind, now you give her o'er. *135*

Lysander. Demetrius loves her, and he loves not you.

---

114 *fond pageant* foolish exhibition   119 *alone* unique, supreme
127 *badge of faith* (Lysander means his tears)   128 *advance* ex-
hibit, display

Demetrius. [*Awaking*] O Helen, goddess, nymph, per-
        fect, divine!
    To what, my love, shall I compare thine eyne?
    Crystal is muddy. O, how ripe in show°
140 Thy lips, those kissing cherries, tempting grow!
    That pure congealèd white, high Taurus'° snow,
    Fanned with the eastern wind, turns to a crow
    When thou hold'st up thy hand: O, let me kiss
    This princess of pure white, this seal of bliss!

145 *Helena.* O spite! O hell! I see you all are bent
    To set against me for your merriment:
    If you were civil° and knew courtesy,
    You would not do me thus much injury.
    Can you not hate me, as I know you do,
150 But you must join in souls to mock me too?
    If you were men, as men you are in show,
    You would not use a gentle° lady so;
    To vow, and swear, and superpraise my parts,°
    When I am sure you hate me with your hearts.
155 You both are rivals, and love Hermia;
    And now both rivals to mock Helena:
    A trim° exploit, a manly enterprise,
    To conjure tears up in a poor maid's eyes
    With your derision! None of noble sort
160 Would so offend a virgin, and extort°
    A poor soul's patience, all to make you sport.

Lysander. You are unkind, Demetrius. Be not so;
    For you love Hermia; this you know I know.
    And here, with all good will, with all my heart,
165 In Hermia's love I yield you up my part;
    And yours of Helena to me bequeath,
    Whom I do love, and will do till my death.

Helena. Never did mockers waste more idle° breath.

Demetrius. Lysander, keep thy Hermia; I will none.

139 *show* appearance 141 *Taurus'* of the Taurus Mountains (in
Turkey) 147 *civil* civilized 152 *gentle* well-born 153 *parts* qualities 157 *trim* splendid (ironical) 160 *extort* wear out by torturing 168 *idle* vain, futile

If e'er I loved her, all that love is gone.   *170*
My heart to her but as guestwise sojourned,
And now to Helen is it home returned,
There to remain.

Lysander.   Helen, it is not so.

Demetrius. Disparage not the faith thou dost not
     know,
Lest, to thy peril, thou aby it dear.°   *175*
Look, where thy love comes; yonder is thy dear.

Enter Hermia.

Hermia. Dark night, that from the eye his° function
     takes,
The ear more quick of apprehension makes;
Wherein it doth impair the seeing sense,
It pays the hearing double recompense.   *180*
Thou art not by mine eye, Lysander, found;
Mine ear, I thank it, brought me to thy sound.
But why unkindly didst thou leave me so?

Lysander. Why should he stay, whom love doth press
     to go?

Hermia. What love could press Lysander from my
     side?   *185*

Lysander. Lysander's love, that would not let him
     bide,
Fair Helena, who more engilds the night
Than all yon fiery oes° and eyes of light.
Why seek'st thou me? Could not this make thee
     know,
The hate I bare thee made me leave thee so?   *190*

Hermia. You speak not as you think: it cannot be.

Helena. Lo, she is one of this confederacy!
Now I perceive they have conjoined all three

175 *aby it dear* pay dearly for it   177 *his* its (the eye's)   188 *oes*
orbs

To fashion this false sport, in spite of me.
195   Injurious° Hermia! Most ungrateful maid!
Have you conspired, have you with these contrived
To bait° me with this foul derision?
Is all the counsel that we two have shared,
The sister's vows, the hours that we have spent,
200   When we have chid the hasty-footed time
For parting us—O, is all forgot?
All school days friendship, childhood innocence?
We, Hermia, like two artificial° gods,
Have with our needles created both one flower,
Both on one sampler,° sitting on one cushion,
Both warbling of one song, both in one key;
As if our hands, our sides, voices, and minds,
Had been incorporate.° So we grew together,
Like to a double cherry, seeming parted,
210   But yet an union in partition;
Two lovely berries molded on one stem;
So, with two seeming bodies, but one heart;
Two of the first, like coats in heraldry,
Due but to one, and crownèd with one crest.°
215   And will you rent° our ancient love asunder,
To join with men in scorning your poor friend?
It is not friendly, 'tis not maidenly.
Our sex, as well as I, may chide you for it,
Though I alone do feel the injury.

220   *Hermia.* I am amazèd at your passionate words.
I scorn you not. It seems that you scorn me.

Helena. Have you not set Lysander, as in scorn,
To follow me and praise my eyes and face?
And made your other love, Demetrius
225   (Who even but now did spurn me with his foot),
To call me goddess, nymph, divine and rare,

---

195 *Injurious* insulting   196–97 *contrived To bait* plotted to assail
203 *artificial* skilled in art   205 *sampler* work of embroidery
208 *incorporate* one body   213–14 *Two of . . . one crest* (Helena
apparently envisages a shield on which the coat of arms appears
twice but which has a single crest; Helena and Hermia have two
bodies but a single heart)   215 *rent* rend, tear

Precious, celestial? Wherefore speaks he this
To her he hates? And wherefore doth Lysander
Deny your love,° so rich within his soul,
And tender me (forsooth) affection,   230
But by your setting on, by your consent?
What though I be not so in grace° as you,
So hung upon with love, so fortunate,
But miserable most, to love unloved?
This you should pity rather than despise.   235

Hermia. I understand not what you mean by this.

Helena. Ay, do! Persever,° counterfeit sad° looks,
Make mouths° upon me when I turn my back;
Wink each at other; hold the sweet jest up.
This sport, well carried, shall be chronicled.   240
If you have any pity, grace, or manners,
You would not make me such an argument.°
But fare ye well. 'Tis partly my own fault,
Which death or absence soon shall remedy.

Lysander. Stay, gentle Helena; hear my excuse: 245
My love, my life, my soul, fair Helena!

Helena. O excellent!

Hermia.   Sweet, do not scorn her so.

Demetrius. If she cannot entreat,° I can compel.

Lysander. Thou canst compel no more than she en-
treat.
Thy threats have no more strength than her weak
prayers.   250
Helen, I love thee; by my life, I do!
I swear by that which I will lose for thee,
To prove him false that says I love thee not.

Demetrius. I say I love thee more than he can do.

---

229 *your love* his love for you   232 *in grace* in favor   237 *persever*
persevere (but accented on second syllable)   237 *sad* grave
238 *Make mouths* make mocking faces   242 *argument* subject (of
scorn)   248 *entreat* prevail by entreating

255 *Lysander.* If thou say so, withdraw and prove it too.

Demetrius. Quick, come!

Hermia.   Lysander, whereto tends all this?

Lysander. Away, you Ethiope!°

Demetrius.   No, no; he'll
  Seem to break loose; take on as° you would follow,
  But yet come not: you are a tame man, go!

Lysander. Hang off, thou cat, thou burr! Vile thing,
260   let loose,
  Or I will shake thee from me like a serpent!

Hermia. Why are you grown so rude! What change is
  this,
  Sweet love?

Lysander.   Thy love! Out, tawny Tartar, out!
  Out, loathèd med'cine! O hated potion, hence!

Hermia. Do you not jest?

265 *Helena.*   Yes, sooth;° and so do you.

Lysander. Demetrius, I will keep my word° with thee.

Demetrius. I would I had your bond, for I perceive
  A weak bond holds you. I'll not trust your word.

Lysander. What, should I hurt her, strike her, kill
  her dead?
270   Although I hate her, I'll not harm her so.

Hermia. What, can you do me greater harm than
  hate?
  Hate me! Wherefore? O me! What news, my love!
  Am not I Hermia? Are not you Lysander?
  I am as fair now as I was erewhile.°

---

257 *Ethiope* blackamoor (brunette)   258 *take on as* make a fuss
as if   265 *sooth* truly   266 *my word* my promise to fight with you
274 *erewhile* a little while ago

Since night° you loved me; yet since night you left
  me.   275
Why, then you left me—O, the gods forbid!—
In earnest, shall I say?

Lysander.   Ay, by my life!
And never did desire to see thee more.
Therefore be out of hope, of question, of doubt;
Be certain, nothing truer. 'Tis no jest   280
That I do hate thee, and love Helena.

Hermia. O me! You juggler! You canker blossom!°
You thief of love! What, have you come by night
And stol'n my love's heart from him?

Helena.   Fine, i' faith!
Have you no modesty, no maiden shame,   285
No touch of bashfulness? What, will you tear
Impatient answers from my gentle tongue?
Fie, fie! You counterfeit, you puppet, you!

Hermia. Puppet? Why so? Ay, that way goes the
  game.
Now I perceive that she hath made compare°   290
Between our statures; she hath urged her height,
And with her personage, her tall personage,
Her height, forsooth, she hath prevailed with him.
And are you grown so high in his esteem,
Because I am so dwarfish and so low?   295
How low am I, thou painted maypole? Speak!
How low am I? I am not yet so low
But that my nails can reach unto thine eyes.

Helena. I pray you, though you mock me, gentlemen,
Let her not hurt me. I was never curst;°   300
I have no gift at all in shrewishness;
I am a right maid° for my cowardice.
Let her not strike me. You perhaps may think,

---

275 *Since night* since the beginning of this night   282 *canker blossom* dog rose (or possibly worm that cankers the blossom)
290 *compare* comparison   300 *curst* quarrelsome   302 *right maid*
true young woman

Because she is something lower than myself,
That I can match her.

305 *Hermia.*   Lower! Hark, again!

Helena. Good Hermia, do not be so bitter with me.
I evermore did love you, Hermia,
Did ever keep your counsels, never wronged you;
Save that, in love unto Demetrius,
310 I told him of your stealth unto this wood.
He followed you; for love I followed him.
But he hath chid me hence, and threatened me
To strike me, spurn me, nay, to kill me too.
And now, so you will let me quiet go,
315 To Athens will I bear my folly back,
And follow you no further. Let me go.
You see how simple and how fond° I am.

Hermia. Why, get you gone. Who is't that hinders you?

Helena. A foolish heart, that I leave here behind.

Hermia. What, with Lysander?

320 *Helena.*   With Demetrius.

Lysander. Be not afraid. She shall not harm thee,
    Helena.

Demetrius. No, sir, she shall not, though you take her
    part.

Helena. O, when she's angry, she is keen and shrewd!°
She was a vixen when she went to school;
325 And though she be but little, she is fierce.

Hermia. "Little" again! Nothing but "low" and "little"!
Why will you suffer her to flout me thus?
Let me come to her.

Lysander.   Get you gone, you dwarf;
You minimus,° of hind'ring knotgrass° made;
You bead, you acorn!

317 *fond* foolish   323 *keen and shrewd* sharp-tongued and shrewish
329 *minimus* smallest thing   329 *knotgrass* (a weed that allegedly
stunted one's growth)

Demetrius.   You are too officious   330
  In her behalf that scorns your services.
  Let her alone. Speak not of Helena;
  Take not her part; for, if thou dost intend°
  Never so little show of love to her,
  Thou shalt aby° it.

Lysander.   Now she holds me not.   335
  Now follow, if thou dar'st, to try whose right,
  Of thine or mine, is most in Helena.

Demetrius. Follow! Nay, I'll go with thee, cheek by
        jowl.   [*Exeunt Lysander and Demetrius.*]

Hermia. You, mistress, all this coil is 'long of you:°
  Nay, go not back.

Helena.   I will not trust you, I,   340
  Nor longer stay in your curst company.
  Your hands than mine are quicker for a fray,
  My legs are longer though, to run away.

Hermia. I am amazed,° and know not what to say.
                    Exeunt [*Helena and Hermia*].

Oberon. This is thy negligence. Still thou mistak'st,   345
  Or else committ'st thy knaveries willfully.

Puck. Believe me, king of shadows, I mistook.
  Did not you tell me I should know the man
  By the Athenian garments he had on?
  And so far blameless proves my enterprise,   350
  That I have 'nointed an Athenian's eyes;
  And so far am I glad it so did sort,°
  As this their jangling I esteem a sport.

Oberon. Thou see'st these lovers seek a place to fight.
  Hie therefore, Robin, overcast the night.   355
  The starry welkin° cover thou anon

---

333 *intend* give sign, direct (or possibly "pretend")   335 *aby* pay
for   339 *all this coil is 'long of you* all this turmoil is brought about
by you   344 *amazed* in confusion   352 *sort* turn out   356 *welkin*
sky

    With drooping fog, as black as Acheron;°
    And lead these testy° rivals so astray,
    As° one come not within another's way.
360   Like to Lysander sometime frame thy tongue,
    Then stir Demetrius up with bitter wrong;°
    And sometime rail thou like Demetrius.
    And from each other look thou lead them thus,
    Till o'er their brows death-counterfeiting sleep
365   With leaden legs and batty° wings doth creep.
    Then crush this herb into Lysander's eye,
    Whose liquor hath this virtuous° property,
    To take from thence all error with his might,
    And make his eyeballs roll with wonted sight.
370   When they next wake, all this derision°
    Shall seem a dream and fruitless vision,
    And back to Athens shall the lovers wend,
    With league whose date° till death shall never end.
    Whiles I in this affair do thee employ,
375   I'll to my queen and beg her Indian boy;
    And then I will her charmèd eye release
    From monster's view, and all things shall be peace.

Puck. My fairy lord, this must be done with haste,
    For night's swift dragons cut the clouds full fast,
380   And yonder shines Aurora's harbinger;°
    At whose approach, ghosts, wand'ring here and there,
    Troop home to churchyards: damnèd spirits all,
    That in crossways and floods have burial,
    Already to their wormy beds are gone.
385   For fear lest day should look their shames upon,
    They willfully themselves exile from light,
    And must for aye consort with black-browed night.

Oberon. But we are spirits of another sort.

---

357 *Acheron* one of the rivers of the underworld   358 *testy*
excited, angry   359 *As* that   361 *wrong* insult   365 *batty* bat-like
367 *virtuous* potent   370 *derision* i.e., ludicrous delusion   373 *With
league whose date* in union whose term   380 *Aurora's harbinger*
dawn's herald (i.e., the morning star)

I with the Morning's love° have oft made sport;
And, like a forester, the groves may tread,   390
Even till the eastern gate, all fiery-red,
Opening on Neptune with fair blessèd beams,
Turns into yellow gold his salt green streams.
But, notwithstanding, haste; make no delay.
We may effect this business yet ere day.   *[Exit.]*   395

Puck.   Up and down, up and down,
                 I will lead them up and down:
                 I am feared in field and town:
                 Goblin,° lead them up and down.
                 Here comes one.   400

Enter Lysander.

Lysander. Where art thou, proud Demetrius? Speak
   thou now.

Puck. Here, villain; drawn° and ready. Where art
   thou?

Lysander. I will be with thee straight.

Puck.   Follow me, then,
       To plainer° ground.   *[Exit Lysander.]*

Enter Demetrius.

Demetrius.   Lysander! Speak again!
   Thou runaway, thou coward, art thou fled?   405
   Speak! In some bush? Where dost thou hide thy
   head?

Puck. Thou coward, art thou bragging to the stars,
   Telling the bushes that thou look'st for wars,
   And wilt not come? Come, recreant! Come, thou
   child!

389 *the Morning's love* Aurora (or possibly her lover Cephalus)
399 *Goblin* Hobgoblin (one of Puck's names)   402 *drawn* with
drawn sword   404 *plainer* more level

410 I'll whip thee with a rod. He is defiled
That draws a sword on thee.

Demetrius.   Yea, art thou there?

Puck. Follow my voice. We'll try no manhood° here.
                              Exeunt.

[*Enter Lysander.*]

Lysander. He goes before me and still dares me on:
When I come where he calls, then he is gone.
415 The villain is much lighter-heeled than I.
I followed fast, but faster he did fly,
That fallen am I in dark uneven way,
And here will rest me. [*Lies down.*] Come, thou
gentle day!
For if but once thou show me thy gray light,
420 I'll find Demetrius, and revenge this spite. [*Sleeps.*]

[*Enter*] *Robin* [*Puck*] *and Demetrius.*

Puck. Ho, ho, ho! Coward, why com'st thou not?

Demetrius. Abide me,° if thou dar'st; for well I wot°
Thou runn'st before me, shifting every place,
And dar'st not stand, nor look me in the face
Where art thou now?

425 *Puck.*   Come hither. I am here.

Demetrius. Nay, then, thou mock'st me. Thou shalt
buy this dear,°
If ever I thy face by daylight see.
Now, go thy way. Faintness constraineth me
To measure out my length on this cold bed.
430 By day's approach look to be visited.°
                              [*Lies down and sleeps.*]

---

412 *try no manhood* have no test of valor   422 *Abide me* wait for
me   422 *wot* know   426 *buy this dear* pay dearly for this   430 *look
to be visited* be sure to be sought out

Enter Helena.

Helena. O weary night, O long and tedious night,
   Abate° thy hours! Shine comforts from the east,
That I may back to Athens by daylight,
   From these that my poor company detest:
And sleep, that sometimes shuts up sorrow's eye,   435
Steal me awhile from mine own company.   *Sleep.*

   Puck.   Yet but three? Come one more.
           Two of both kinds makes up four.
           Here she comes, curst° and sad:
           Cupid is a knavish lad,   440
           Thus to make poor females mad.

[*Enter Hermia.*]

Hermia. Never so weary, never so in woe;
   Bedabbled with the dew and torn with briers,
I can no further crawl, no further go;
   My legs can keep no pace with my desires.   445
Here will I rest me till the break of day.
Heavens shield Lysander, if they mean a fray!
                [*Lies down and sleeps.*]

Puck. On the ground
      Sleep sound:
      I'll apply   450
      To your eye,
   Gentle lover, remedy.
        [*Squeezing the juice on Lysander's eye*]
      When thou wak'st,
      Thou tak'st
      True delight   455
      In the sight
Of thy former lady's eye:
And the country proverb known,
That every man should take his own,

460 In your waking shall be shown.
    Jack shall have Jill;
    Nought shall go ill;
The man shall have his mare again, and all shall
  be well.

                            [*Exit.*]

[ACT IV

Scene I. *The wood. Lysander, Demetrius, Helena, and Hermia, lying asleep.*]

Enter [Titania,] Queen of Fairies, and [Bottom the] Clown, and Fairies; and [Oberon,] the King, behind them.

Titania. Come, sit thee down upon this flow'ry bed,
While I thy amiable cheeks do coy,°
And stick musk roses in thy sleek smooth head,
And kiss thy fair large ears, my gentle joy.

Bottom. Where's Peaseblossom?   5

Peaseblossom. Ready.

Bottom. Scratch my head, Peaseblossom. Where's Mounsieur Cobweb?

Cobweb. Ready.

Bottom. Mounsieur Cobweb, good mounsieur, get   10
you your weapons in your hand, and kill me a red-
hipped humblebee on the top of a thistle; and, good
mounsieur, bring me the honey bag. Do not fret
yourself too much in the action, mounsieur; and,
good mounsieur, have a care the honey bag break   15

IV.i.2 *While I . . . do coy* while I caress your lovely cheeks

not; I would be loath to have you overflown with
a honey bag, signior. Where's Mounsieur Mustardseed?

Mustardseed. Ready.

20   *Bottom.* Give me your neaf,° Mounsieur Mustardseed. Pray you, leave your curtsy,° good mounsieur.

Mustardseed. What's your will?

Bottom. Nothing, good mounsieur, but to help Cava-
25   lery° Cobweb to scratch. I must to the barber's,
mounsieur; for methinks I am marvail's° hairy
about the face; and I am such a tender ass, if my
hair do but tickle me, I must scratch.

Titania. What, wilt thou hear some music, my sweet
30   love?

Bottom. I have a reasonable good ear in music. Let's
have the tongs and the bones.°

Titania. Or say, sweet love, what thou desirest to eat.

Bottom. Truly, a peck of provender. I could munch
35   your good dry oats. Methinks I have a great desire
to a bottle° of hay. Good hay, sweet hay, hath no
fellow.°

Titania. I have a venturous fairy that shall seek
The squirrel's hoard, and fetch thee new nuts.

40   *Bottom.* I had rather have a handful or two of dried
peas. But, I pray you, let none of your people stir
me: I have an exposition of° sleep come upon me.

---

20 *neaf* fist, hand   21 *leave your curtsy* i.e., stop bowing, leave your
hat on (a curtsy was any gesture of respect)   24–25 *Cavalery* i.e.,
Cavalier   26 *marvail's* (Bottom means "marvelous")   32 *the tongs
and the bones* rustic music, made by tongs struck with metal and by
bone clappers held between the fingers   36 *bottle* bundle   37 *fellow*
equal   42 *exposition of* (Bottom means "disposition for")

Titania. Sleep thou, and I will wind thee in my arms.
Fairies, be gone, and be all ways° away.

                  [Exeunt Fairies.]

So doth the woodbine the sweet honeysuckle   *45*
Gently entwist; the female ivy° so
Enrings the barky fingers of the elm.
O, how I love thee! How I dote on thee!

                    [They sleep.]

      Enter Robin Goodfellow [Puck].

Oberon. [*Advancing*] Welcome, good Robin. See'st
thou this sweet sight?
Her dotage now I do begin to pity: *50*
For, meeting her of late behind the wood,
Seeking sweet favors° for this hateful fool,
I did upbraid her, and fall out with her.
For she his hairy temples then had rounded
With coronet of fresh and fragrant flowers;   *55*
And that same dew, which sometime° on the buds
Was wont° to swell, like round and orient° pearls,
Stood now within the pretty flouriets'° eyes,
Like tears, that did their own disgrace bewail.
When I had at my pleasure taunted her,   *60*
And she in mild terms begged my patience,
I then did ask of her her changeling child;
Which straight she gave me, and her fairy sent
To bear him to my bower in fairy land.
And now I have the boy, I will undo   *65*
This hateful imperfection of her eyes:
And, gentle Puck, take this transformèd scalp
From off the head of this Athenian swain,
That, he awaking when the other° do,
May all to Athens back again repair,   *70*
And think no more of this night's accidents,°

44 *all ways* in every direction   46 *female ivy* (called female because
it clings to the elm and is supported by it)   52 *favors* love tokens
(probably flowers)   56 *sometime* formerly   57 *Was wont* used to
57 *orient* lustrous   58 *flouriets'* flowerets'   69 *other* others   71 *ac-cidents* happenings

But as the fierce vexation of a dream.
But first I will release the Fairy Queen.
   Be as thou wast wont to be;
75   See as thou wast wont to see.
   Dian's bud o'er Cupid's flower
   Hath such force and blessèd power.
Now, my Titania, wake you, my sweet Queen.

Titania. My Oberon, what visions have I seen!
80   Methought I was enamored of an ass.

Oberon. There lies your love.

Titania.   How came these things to pass?
   O, how mine eyes do loathe his visage now!

Oberon. Silence awhile. Robin, take off this head.
   Titania, music call; and strike more dead
85   Than common sleep of all these five the sense.

Titania. Music, ho, music! Such as charmeth sleep!

Puck. Now, when thou wak'st, with thine own fool's
   eyes peep.

Oberon. Sound, music! [*Music*] Come, my Queen,
   take hands with me,
And rock the ground whereon these sleepers be.
                   [*Dance*]
90   Now thou and I are new in amity,
And will tomorrow midnight solemnly°
Dance in Duke Theseus' house triumphantly,°
And bless it to all fair prosperity.
There shall the pairs of faithful lovers be
95   Wedded, with Theseus, all in jollity.

Puck.   Fairy King, attend, and mark:
   I do hear the morning lark.

Oberon.   Then, my Queen, in silence sad,°
   Trip we after night's shade.

---

91 *solemnly* ceremoniously   92 *triumphantly* in festive procession
98 *sad* serious, solemn

> We the globe can compass soon,   *100*
> Swifter than the wand'ring moon.

Titania.   Come, my lord; and in our flight,
> Tell me how it came this night,
> That I sleeping here was found
> With these mortals on the ground.   *105*

Exeunt.

Wind horn. Enter Theseus, and all his train;
[Hippolyta, Egeus].

Theseus. Go, one of you, find out the forester,
> For now our observation° is performed;
> And since we have the vaward° of the day,
> My love shall hear <u>the music of my hounds</u>.
> Uncouple in the western valley; let them go.   *110*
> Dispatch, I say, and find the forester.

[Exit an Attendant.]

> We will, fair Queen, up to the mountain's top,
> And mark the musical confusion
> Of hounds and echo in conjunction.

Hippolyta. I was with Hercules and Cadmus once,   *115*
> When in a wood of Crete they bayed° the bear
> With hounds of Sparta. Never did I hear
> Such gallant chiding; for, besides the groves,
> The skies, the fountains, every region near
> Seemed all one mutual cry. I never heard   *120*
> <u>So musical a discord,</u> such sweet thunder.

Theseus. My hounds are bred out of the Spartan kind,
> So flewed, so sanded;° and their heads are hung
> With ears that sweep away the morning dew;
> Crook-kneed, and dew-lapped like Thessalian bulls;   *125*
> Slow in pursuit, but matched in mouth like bells,

(handwritten annotations: "statement as to nature of music"; "as opposed to harmony"; "Music is different things for different people.")

---

107 *observation* observance, i.e., of the rite of May (cf. I.i.167)
108 *vaward* vanguard, i.e., morning   116 *bayed* brought to bay
123 *So flewed, so sanded* i.e., like Spartan hounds, with hanging cheeks and of sandy color

Each under each.° A cry° more tunable
Was never holloed to, nor cheered with horn,
In Crete, in Sparta, nor in Thessaly.
Judge when you hear. But, soft!° What nymphs
130 are these?

Egeus. My lord, this is my daughter here asleep;
And this, Lysander; this Demetrius is;
This Helena, old Nedar's Helena:
I wonder of their being here together.

135 *Theseus.* No doubt they rose up early to observe
The rite of May; and, hearing our intent,
Came here in grace of our solemnity.°
But speak, Egeus. Is not this the day
That Hermia should give answer of her choice?

140 *Egeus.* It is, my lord.

Theseus. Go, bid the huntsmen wake them with their
 horns.

   Shout within. They all start up. Wind horns.

Good morrow, friends. Saint Valentine is past:
Begin these wood birds but to couple now?°

Lysander. Pardon, my lord.

Theseus.   I pray you all, stand up.
145 I know you two are rival enemies.
How comes this gentle concord in the world,
That hatred is so far from jealousy,°
To sleep by hate, and fear no enmity?

Lysander. My lord, I shall reply amazedly,°
150 Half sleep, half waking: but as yet, I swear,
I cannot truly say how I came here.

---

127 *Each under each* of different tone (like the chime of bells)
127 *cry* pack of hounds 130 *soft* stop 137 *in grace of our solemnity* in honor of our festival 143 *Begin these . . . couple now* (it
was supposed that birds began to mate on February 14, St. Valentine's Day) 147 *jealousy* suspicion 149 *amazedly* confusedly

But, as I think—for truly would I speak,
And now I do bethink me, so it is—
I came with Hermia hither. Our intent
Was to be gone from Athens, where we might,   *155*
Without° the peril of the Athenian law—

Egeus. Enough, enough, my lord; you have enough.
I beg the law, the law, upon his head.
They would have stol'n away; they would, Deme-
    trius,
Thereby to have defeated° you and me,   *160*
You of your wife and me of my consent,
Of my consent that she should be your wife.

Demetrius. My lord, fair Helen told me of their
    stealth,°
Of this their purpose hither to this wood,
And I in fury hither followed them,   *165*
Fair Helena in fancy° following me.
But, my good lord, I wot not by what power—
But by some power it is—my love to Hermia,
Melted as the snow, seems to me now
As the remembrance of an idle gaud,°   *170*
Which in my childhood I did dote upon;
And all the faith, the virtue° of my heart,
The object and the pleasure of mine eye,
Is only Helena. To her, my lord,
Was I betrothed ere I saw Hermia: *175*
But, like a sickness,° did I loathe this food;
But, as in health, come to my natural taste,
Now I do wish it, love it, long for it,
And will for evermore be true to it.

Theseus. Fair lovers, you are fortunately met.   *180*
Of this discourse we more will hear anon.
Egeus, I will overbear your will,
For in the temple, by and by,° with us

156 *Without* outside of   160 *defeated* deprived by fraud   163
stealth stealthy flight   166 *in fancy* in love, doting   170 *idle gaud*
worthless trinket   172 *virtue* power   176 *like a sickness* like one
who is sick   183 *by and by* shortly

These couples shall eternally be knit;
185 And, for the morning now is something worn,°
Our purposed hunting shall be set aside.
Away with us to Athens! Three and three,
We'll hold a feast in great solemnity.
Come, Hippolyta.
       [*Exeunt Theseus, Hippolyta, Egeus, and train.*]

Demetrius. These things seem small and undistin-
190   guishable,
Like far-off mountains turnèd into clouds.

Hermia. Methinks I see these things with parted eye,°
When everything seems double.

Helena.   So methinks:
And I have found Demetrius like a jewel,
Mine own, and not mine own.

195 *Demetrius.*   Are you sure
That we are awake? It seems to me
That yet we sleep, we dream. Do not you think
The Duke was here, and bid us follow him?

Hermia. Yea, and my father.

Helena.   And Hippolyta.

200 *Lysander.* And he did bid us follow to the temple.

Demetrius. Why, then, we are awake. Let's follow
       him,
And by the way let us recount our dreams.
                                    [*Exeunt.*]

Bottom. [*Awaking*] When my cue comes, call me,
and I will answer. My next is, "Most fair Pyramus."
205   Heigh-ho! Peter Quince? Flute, the bellows
mender? Snout, the tinker? Starveling? God's my
life,° stol'n hence, and left me asleep? I have had
a most rare vision. I have had a dream, past the

---

185 *something worn* somewhat spent   192 *with parted eye* i.e., with
the eyes out of focus   206–07 *God's my life* an oath (possibly from
"God bless my life")

wit of man to say what dream it was. Man is but
an ass, if he go about° to expound this dream.   210
Methought I was—there is no man can tell what.
Methought I was—and methought I had—but man
is but a patched° fool if he will offer to say what
methought I had. The eye of man hath not heard,
the ear of man hath not seen, man's hand is not   215
able to taste, his tongue to conceive, nor his heart
to report, what my dream was. I will get Peter
Quince to write a ballet° of this dream. It shall
be called "Bottom's Dream," because it hath no
bottom; and I will sing it in the latter end of a   220
play, before the Duke. Peradventure to make it
the more gracious, I shall sing it at her death.°

                                        [*Exit.*]

[*Scene II.   Athens. Quince's house.*]

Enter Quince, Flute,° Thisby and the rabble
            [*Snout, Starveling*].

Quince. Have you sent to Bottom's house? Is he come
    home yet?

Starveling. He cannot be heard of. Out of doubt he
    is transported.°

Flute. If he come not, then the play is marred. It   5
    goes not forward, doth it?

Quince. It is not possible. You have not a man in all

---

210 *go about* endeavor   213 *patched* (referring to the patchwork
dress of jesters)   218 *ballet* ballad   222 *her death* i.e., Thisby's
death in the play   IV.ii.s.d. *Flute* (Shakespeare seems to have for-
gotten that Flute and Thisby are the same person)   4 *transported*
carried off (by the fairies)

Athens able to discharge° Pyramus but he.

Flute. No, he hath simply the best wit of any handi-
craft man in Athens.

Quince. Yea, and the best person too; and he is a
very paramour for a sweet voice.

Flute. You must say "paragon." A paramour is, God
bless us, a thing of nought.°

Enter Snug the Joiner.

Snug. Masters, the Duke is coming from the temple,
and there is two or three lords and ladies more
married. If our sport had gone forward, we had
all been made men.°

Flute. O sweet bully Bottom! Thus hath he lost sixpence a day° during his life. He could not have
scaped sixpence a day. An the Duke had not given
him sixpence a day for playing Pyramus, I'll be
hanged. He would have deserved it. Sixpence a
day in Pyramus, or nothing.

Enter Bottom.

Bottom. Where are these lads? Where are these
hearts?

Quince. Bottom! O most courageous° day! O most
happy hour!

Bottom. Masters, I am to discourse wonders: but ask
me not what; for if I tell you, I am not true
Athenian. I will tell you everything, right as it fell
out.

Quince. Let us hear, sweet Bottom.

---

8 *discharge* play   14 *a thing of nought* a wicked thing   18 *made
men* men whose fortunes are made   19–20 *sixpence a day* (a pen-
sion)   27 *courageous* brave, splendid

Bottom. Not a word of me.° All that I will tell you
is, that the Duke hath dined. Get your apparel   35
together, good strings to your beards, new ribbons
to your pumps; meet presently° at the palace; every
man look o'er his part; for the short and the long
is, our play is preferred.° In any case, let Thisby
have clean linen; and let not him that plays the   40
lion pare his nails, for they shall hang out for the
lion's claws. And, most dear actors, eat no onions
nor garlic, for we are to utter sweet breath,° and
I do not doubt but to hear them say it is a sweet
comedy. No more words. Away! Go, away!   45

                              [*Exeunt.*]

---

34 *of me* from me   37 *presently* immediately   39 *preferred* put
forward, recommended   43 *breath* (1) exhalation (2) words

[ACT V

Scene I. *Athens. The palace of Theseus.*]

Enter Theseus, Hippolyta, and Philostrate, [Lords, and Attendants].

Hippolyta. 'Tis strange, my Theseus, that these lovers speak of.

Theseus. More strange than true. I never may believe
These antique° fables, nor these fairy toys.°
Lovers and madmen have such seething brains,
5   Such shaping fantasies,° that apprehend
More than cool reason ever comprehends.
The lunatic, the lover and the poet
Are of imagination all compact.°
One sees more devils than vast hell can hold,
10   That is the madman. The lover, all as frantic,
Sees Helen's beauty in a brow of Egypt.°
The poet's eye, in a fine frenzy rolling,
Doth glance from heaven to earth, from earth to heaven;
And as imagination bodies forth
15   The forms of things unknown, the poet's pen
Turns them to shapes, and gives to airy nothing
A local habitation and a name.

V.i.3 *antique* (1) ancient (2) grotesque (antic)   3 *fairy toys* trifles about fairies   5 *fantasies* imagination   8 *compact* composed   11 *brow of Egypt* face of a gypsy

Such tricks hath strong imagination,
That, if it would but apprehend some joy,
It comprehends some bringer of that joy;°   *20*
Or in the night, imagining some fear,°
How easy is a bush supposed a bear!

Hippolyta. But all the story of the night told over,
And all their minds transfigured so together,
More witnesseth than fancy's images,   *25*
And grows to something of great constancy;°
But, howsoever, strange and admirable.°

*Enter Lovers: Lysander, Demetrius, Hermia and
Helena.*

Theseus. Here come the lovers, full of joy and mirth.
Joy, gentle friends! Joy and fresh days of love
Accompany your hearts!

Lysander.   More than to us   *30*
Wait in your royal walks, your board, your bed!

Theseus. Come now, what masques,° what dances
    shall we have,
To wear away this long age of three hours
Between our aftersupper° and bedtime?
Where is our usual manager of mirth?   *35*
What revels are in hand? Is there no play,
To ease the anguish of a torturing hour?
Call Philostrate.

Philostrate.   Here, mighty Theseus.

Theseus. Say, what abridgment° have you for this
    evening?

20 *It comprehends . . . that joy* it includes an imagined bringer of
the joy   21 *fear* object of fear   26 *constancy* consistency (and
reality)   27 *admirable* wonderful   32 *masques* courtly entertainments with masked dancers   34 *aftersupper* refreshment served
after early supper   39 *abridgment* entertainment (to abridge or
shorten the time)

40   What masque? What music? How shall we beguile
The lazy time, if not with some delight?

Philostrate. There is a brief° how many sports are
ripe:°
Make choice of which your Highness will see first.
[Giving a paper]

Theseus. "The battle with the Centaurs, to be sung
45   By an Athenian eunuch to the harp."
We'll none of that. That have I told my love,
In glory of my kinsman Hercules.
"The riot of the tipsy Bacchanals,
Tearing the Thracian singer° in their rage."
50   That is an old device;° and it was played
When I from Thebes came last a conqueror.
"The thrice three Muses mourning for the death
Of Learning, late deceased in beggary."
That is some satire, keen and critical,
55   Not sorting with° a nuptial ceremony.
"A tedious brief scene of young Pyramus
And his love Thisby; very tragical mirth."
Merry and tragical? Tedious and brief?
That is, hot ice and wondrous strange snow.
60   How shall we find the concord of this discord?

Philostrate. A play there is, my lord, some ten words
long,
Which is as brief as I have known a play;
But by ten words, my lord, it is too long,
Which makes it tedious. For in all the play
65   There is not one word apt, one player fitted.
And tragical, my noble lord, it is,
For Pyramus therein doth kill himself.
Which, when I saw rehearsed, I must confess,
Made mine eyes water; but more merry tears
70   The passion° of loud laughter never shed.

Theseus. What are they that do play it?

42 *brief* written list   42 *ripe* ready to be presented   49 *Thracian
singer* Orpheus   50 *device* show   55 *sorting with* suited to   70 *passion* strong emotion

Philostrate. Hard-handed men, that work in Athens
   here,
   Which never labored in their minds till now;
   And now have toiled their unbreathed° memories
   With this same play, against° your nuptial.   75

Theseus. And we will hear it.

Philostrate.   No, my noble lord;
   It is not for you. I have heard it over,
   And it is nothing, nothing in the world;
   Unless you can find sport in their intents,
   Extremely stretched and conned with cruel pain,   80
   To do you service.

Theseus.   I will hear that play;
   For never anything can be amiss,
   When simpleness and duty tender it.
   Go, bring them in: and take your places, ladies.
                              [*Exit Philostrate.*]

Hippolyta. I love not to see wretchedness o'ercharged,°   85
   And duty in his service perishing.

Theseus. Why, gentle sweet, you shall see no such
   thing.

Hippolyta. He says they can do nothing in this kind.°

Theseus. The kinder we, to give them thanks for
   nothing.
   Our sport shall be to take what they mistake: 90
   And what poor duty cannot do, noble respect
   Takes it in might,° not merit.
   Where I have come, great clerks° have purposèd
   To greet me with premeditated welcomes;
   Where I have seen them shiver and look pale,   95
   Make periods in the midst of sentences,
   Throttle their practiced accent in their fears,

---

74 *unbreathed* unexercised   75 *against* in preparation for   85
wretchedness o'ercharged lowly people overburdened   88 *in this
kind* in this kind of thing (i.e., acting)   92 *Takes it in might* con-
siders the ability and the effort made   93 *clerks* scholars

And, in conclusion, dumbly have broke off,
Not paying me a welcome. Trust me, sweet,
100 Out of this silence yet I picked a welcome;
And in the modesty of fearful duty
I read as much as from the rattling tongue
Of saucy and audacious eloquence.
Love, therefore, and tongue-tied simplicity
105 In least speak most, to my capacity.°

[*Enter Philostrate.*]

Philostrate. So please your Grace, the Prologue is
addressed.°

Theseus. Let him approach.   [*Flourish trumpets.*]

Enter the Prologue [*Quince*].

Prologue. If we offend, it is with our good will.
That you should think, we come not to offend,
110 But with good will. To show our simple skill,
That is the true beginning of our end.°
Consider, then, we come but in despite.
We do not come, as minding to content you,
Our true intent is. All for your delight,
We are not here. That you should here repent
115 you,
The actors are at hand; and, by their show,°
You shall know all, that you are like to know.

Theseus. This fellow doth not stand upon points.°

Lysander. He hath rid his prologue like a rough colt;
120 he knows not the stop.° A good moral, my lord:
it is not enough to speak, but to speak true.

---

105 *to my capacity* according to my understanding   106 *addressed*
ready   111 *end* aim   116 *show* (probably referring to a kind of
pantomime—"dumb show"—that was to follow, in which the
action of the play was acted without words while the Prologue gave
his account)   118 *stand upon points* (1) care about punctuation
(2) worry about niceties   120 *stop* (1) technical term for the check-
ing of a horse (2) mark of punctuation

Hippolyta. Indeed he hath played on this prologue
like a child on a recorder;° a sound, but not in
government.°

Theseus. His speech was like a tangled chain; noth- 125
ing impaired, but all disordered. Who is next?

*Enter Pyramus and Thisby and Wall and Moonshine
and Lion [as in dumbshow].*

Prologue. Gentles, perchance you wonder at this show;
    But wonder on, till truth make all things plain.
This man is Pyramus, if you would know;
    This beauteous lady Thisby is certain. 130
This man, with lime and roughcast, doth present
    Wall, that vile Wall which did these lovers
      sunder;
And through Wall's chink, poor souls, they are
      content
    To whisper. At the which let no man wonder.
This man, with lantern, dog, and bush of thorn, 135
    Presenteth Moonshine; for, if you will know,
By moonshine did these lovers think no scorn
    To meet at Ninus' tomb, there, there to woo.
This grisly beast, which Lion hight° by name,
    The trusty Thisby, coming first by night, 140
Did scare away, or rather did affright;
    And, as she fled, her mantle she did fall,°
Which Lion vile with bloody mouth did stain.
Anon comes Pyramus, sweet youth and tall,°
    And finds his trusty Thisby's mantle slain: 145
Whereat, with blade, with bloody blameful blade,
    He bravely broached° his boiling bloody breast;
And Thisby, tarrying in mulberry shade,
    His dagger drew, and died. For all the rest,

123 *recorder* flutelike instrument 124 *government* control 139
hight is called 142 *fall* let fall 144 *tall* brave 147 *bravely
broached* gallantly stabbed

150   Let Lion, Moonshine, Wall, and lovers twain
  At large° discourse, while here they do remain.

Theseus. I wonder if the lion be to speak.

Demetrius. No wonder, my lord. One lion may, when many asses do.

   Exit Lion, Thisby and Moonshine.

155   *Wall.* In this same interlude it doth befall
  That I, one Snout by name, present a wall;
  And such a wall, as I would have you think,
  That had in it a crannied hole or chink,
  Through which the lovers, Pyramus and Thisby,
160   Did whisper often very secretly.
  This loam, this roughcast, and this stone, doth show
  That I am that same wall; the truth is so;
  And this the cranny is, right and sinister,°
  Through which the fearful lovers are to whisper.

165   *Theseus.* Would you desire lime and hair to speak better?

Demetrius. It is the wittiest partition° that ever I heard discourse, my lord.

Theseus. Pyramus draws near the wall. Silence!

Pyramus. O grim-looked night! O night with hue so
170   black!
  O night, which ever art when day is not!
  O night, O night! Alack, alack, alack,
  I fear my Thisby's promise is forgot!
  And thou, O wall, O sweet, O lovely wall,
  That stand'st between her father's ground and
175   mine!
  Thou wall, O wall, O sweet and lovely wall,

151 *At large* at length 163 *right and sinister* i.e., running right and left, horizontal 167 *wittiest partition* most intelligent wall (with a pun on "partition," a section of a book or of an oration)

Show me thy chink, to blink through with mine
   eyne!

> [*Wall holds up his fingers.*]

Thanks, courteous wall. Jove shield thee well for
   this!
But what see I? No Thisby do I see.
O wicked wall, through whom I see no bliss!   180
   Cursed be thy stones for thus deceiving me!

Theseus. The wall, methinks, being sensible,° should
   curse again.°

Pyramus. No, in truth, sir, he should not. "Deceiving
   me" is Thisby's cue. She is to enter now, and I   185
   am to spy her through the wall. You shall see it
   will fall pat° as I told you. Yonder she comes.

Enter Thisby.

Thisby. O wall, full often hast thou heard my moans,
   For parting my fair Pyramus and me!
My cherry lips have often kissed thy stones,   190
   Thy stones with lime and hair knit up in thee.

Pyramus. I see a voice: now will I to the chink,
   To spy an I can hear my Thisby's face.
   Thisby!

Thisby. My love thou art, my love I think.   195

Pyramus. Think what thou wilt, I am thy lover's
   grace;°
   And, like Limander,° am I trusty still.

Thisby. And I like Helen,° till the Fates me kill.

Pyramus. Not Shafalus to Procrus° was so true.

---

182 *sensible* conscious   183 *again* in return   187 *pat* exactly   196
thy lover's grace thy gracious lover   197 *Limander* (Bottom means
Leander, but blends him with Alexander)   198 *Helen* (Hero, beloved of Leander, is probably meant)   199 *Shafalus to Procrus*
(Cephalus and Procris are meant, legendary lovers)

200 *Thisby.* As Shafalus to Procrus, I to you.

Pyramus. O kiss me through the hole of this vile wall!

Thisby. I kiss the wall's hole, not your lips at all.

Pyramus. Wilt thou at Ninny's tomb meet me straightway?

Thisby. 'Tide life, 'tide death,° I come without delay.
[*Exeunt Pyramus and Thisby.*]

205 *Wall.* Thus have I, Wall, my part dischargèd so;
And, being done, thus wall away doth go.   [*Exit.*]

Theseus. Now is the moon used° between the two
neighbors.

Demetrius. No remedy, my lord, when walls are so
210   willful to hear without warning.

Hippolyta. This is the silliest stuff that ever I heard.

Theseus. The best in this kind° are but shadows; and
the worst are no worse, if imagination amend them.

Hippolyta. It must be your imagination then, and
215   not theirs.

Theseus. If we imagine no worse of them than they
of themselves, they may pass for excellent men.
Here come two noble beasts in, a man and a lion.

Enter Lion and Moonshine.

Lion. You, ladies, you, whose gentle hearts do fear
The smallest monstrous mouse that creeps on
220   floor,

---

204 *'Tide life, 'tide death* come (betide) life or death   207 *moon
used* (the quartos read thus, the Folio reads *morall downe.* Among
suggested emendations are "mural down," and "moon to see")
209–10 *when walls . . . without warning* i.e., when walls are so eager
to listen without warning the parents (?)   212 *in this kind* of this
sort, i.e., plays (or players?)

May now perchance both quake and tremble here,
  When lion rough in wildest rage doth roar.
Then know that I, as Snug the joiner, am
A lion fell,° nor else no lion's dam;
For, if I should as lion come in strife   225
Into this place, 'twere pity on my life.°

Theseus. A very gentle° beast, and of a good con-
    science.

Demetrius. The very best at a beast, my lord, that
    e'er I saw.   230

Lysander. This lion is a very fox for his valor.

Theseus. True; and a goose for his discretion.

Demetrius. Not so, my lord; for his valor cannot
    carry° his discretion, and the fox carries the goose.

Theseus. His discretion, I am sure, cannot carry his 235
    valor; for the goose carries not the fox. It is well.
    Leave it to his discretion, and let us listen to the
    moon.

Moonshine. This lanthorn° doth the hornèd moon
    present—

Demetrius. He should have worn the horns on his
    head.°   240

Theseus. He is no crescent, and his horns are invisible
    within the circumference.

Moonshine. This lanthorn doth the hornèd moon
    present;
  Myself the man i' th' moon do seem to be.   245

Theseus. This is the greatest error of all the rest.

---

224 *lion fell* fierce lion (perhaps with a pun on *fell* = "skin")
226 *pity on my life* a dangerous thing for me   227 *gentle* gentle-
manly, courteous   234 *carry* carry away   239 *lanthorn* (so spelled,
and perhaps pronounced "lant-horn," because lanterns were commonly made of horn)   240 *horns on his head* (cuckolds were said
to have horns)

The man should be put into the lanthorn. How is
it else the man i' th' moon?

Demetrius. He dares not come there for the candle;
250   for, you see, it is already in snuff.°

Hippolyta. I am aweary of this moon. Would he would
change!

Theseus. It appears, by his small light of discretion,
that he is in the wane; but yet, in courtesy, in all
255   reason, we must stay the time.

Lysander. Proceed, Moon.

Moonshine. All that I have to say is to tell you that
the lanthorn is the moon; I, the man i' th' moon;
this thorn bush, my thorn bush; and this dog, my
260   dog.

Demetrius. Why, all these should be in the lanthorn;
for all these are in the moon. But, silence! Here
comes Thisby.

Enter Thisby.

Thisby. This is old Ninny's tomb. Where is my love?

265 *Lion.* Oh—   [*The lion roars. Thisby runs off.*]

Demetrius. Well roared, Lion.

Theseus. Well run, Thisby.

Hippolyta. Well shone, Moon. Truly, the moon shines
with a good grace.
    [*The Lion shakes Thisby's mantle, and exit.*]

270 *Theseus.* Well moused,° Lion.

Demetrius. And then came Pyramus.

Lysander. And so the lion vanished.

---

250 *in snuff* (1) in need of snuffing (2) resentful   270 *moused*
shaken (like a mouse)

Enter Pyramus.

Pyramus. Sweet Moon, I thank thee for thy sunny
  beams;
  I thank thee, Moon, for shining now so bright;
  For, by thy gracious, golden, glittering gleams,   275
      I trust to take of truest Thisby sight.
          But stay, O spite!°
          But mark, poor knight,
      What dreadful dole° is here!
          Eyes, do you see?   280
          How can it be?
      O dainty duck! O dear!
          Thy mantle good,
          What, stained with blood!
      Approach, ye Furies fell!°   285
          O Fates, come, come,
          Cut thread and thrum;°
      Quail,° crush, conclude, and quell!°

Theseus. This passion, and the death of a dear friend,
  would go near to make a man look sad.   290

Hippolyta. Beshrew° my heart, but I pity the man.

Pyramus. O wherefore, Nature, didst thou lions frame?
  Since lion vile hath here deflow'red my dear:
  Which is—no, no—which was the fairest dame
      That lived, that loved, that liked, that looked
      with cheer.°   295
              Come, tears, confound;
              Out, sword, and wound
          The pap of Pyramus;
              Ay, that left pap,
              Where heart doth hop. [*Stabs himself*.]   300
          Thus die I, thus, thus, thus.
              Now am I dead,

---

277 *spite* vexation   279 *dole* sorrowful thing   285 *fell* fierce
287 *thread and thrum* i.e., everything (*thrum* = the end of the
warp thread)   288 *Quail* destroy   288 *quell* kill   291 *Beshrew*
curse (but a mild word)   295 *cheer* countenance

                    Now am I fled;
                    My soul is in the sky.
305   Tongue, lose thy light;
                    Moon, take thy flight.
                                    [*Exit Moonshine.*]
                    Now die, die, die, die, die.   [*Dies.*]

Demetrius. No die, but an ace,° for him; for he is but
    one.

310 *Lysander.* Less than an ace, man; for he is dead, he is
    nothing.

Theseus. With the help of a surgeon he might yet re-
    cover, and yet prove an ass.

Hippolyta. How chance° Moonshine is gone before
315   Thisby comes back and finds her lover?

Theseus. She will find him by starlight. Here she
    comes; and her passion° ends the play.

                    [*Enter Thisby.*]

Hippolyta. Methinks she should not use a long one
    for such a Pyramus. I hope she will be brief.

320 *Demetrius.* A mote will turn the balance, which Pyra-
    mus, which Thisby, is the better; he for a man,
    God warr'nt us; she for a woman, God bless us!

Lysander. She hath spied him already with those
    sweet eyes.

325 *Demetrius.* And thus she means,° videlicet:

Thisby.   Asleep, my love?
                    What, dead, my dove?
                O Pyramus, arise!
                    Speak, speak. Quite dumb?
330   Dead, dead? A tomb

---

308 *No die, but an ace* not a die (singular of "dice"), but a one-spot
on a die   314 *How chance* how does it come that   317 *passion*
passionate speech   325 *means* laments

> Must cover thy sweet eyes.
>   These lily lips,
>   This cherry nose,
> These yellow cowslip cheeks,
>   Are gone, are gone.   335
>   Lovers, make moan.
> His eyes were green as leeks.
>   O Sisters Three,°
>   Come, come to me,
> With hands as pale as milk;   340
>   Lay them in gore,
>   Since you have shore°
> With shears his thread of silk.
>   Tongue, not a word.
>   Come, trusty sword,   345
> Come, blade, my breast imbrue!°
>   [Stabs herself.]
>   And, farewell, friends.
>   Thus Thisby ends.
>   Adieu, adieu, adieu.   [Dies.]

Theseus. Moonshine and Lion are left to bury the   350
dead.

Demetrius. Ay, and Wall too.

Bottom. [*Starting up*] No, I assure you; the wall is
down that parted their fathers. Will it please you
to see the epilogue, or to hear a Bergomask dance°   355
between two of our company?

Theseus. No epilogue, I pray you; for your play needs
no excuse. Never excuse, for when the players are
all dead, there need none to be blamed. Marry, if
he that writ it had played Pyramus and hanged   360
himself in Thisby's garter, it would have been a
fine tragedy: and so it is, truly; and very notably
discharged. But, come, your Bergomask. Let your
epilogue alone.   [*A dance.*]

338 *Sisters Three* i.e., the three Fates   342 *shore* shorn   346 *imbrue*
stain with blood   355 *Bergomask dance* rustic dance

365 The iron tongue of midnight hath told° twelve.
Lovers, to bed; 'tis almost fairy time.
I fear we shall outsleep the coming morn,
As much as we this night have overwatched.
This palpable-gross° play hath well beguiled
370 The heavy gait of night. Sweet friends, to bed.
A fortnight hold we this solemnity,
In nightly revels and new jollity.   *Exeunt.*

Enter Puck [with a broom].

Puck. Now the hungry lion roars,
        And the wolf behowls the moon;
375 Whilst the heavy plowman snores,
        All with weary task fordone.°
Now the wasted° brands do glow,
        Whilst the screech owl, screeching loud,
Puts the wretch that lies in woe
380   In remembrance of a shroud.
Now it is the time of night,
        That the graves, all gaping wide,
Every one lets forth his sprite,
        In the churchway paths to glide:
385 And we fairies, that do run
        By the triple Hecate's team,°
From the presence of the sun,
        Following darkness like a dream,
Now are frolic.° Not a mouse
390 Shall disturb this hallowed house:
I am sent, with broom, before,
To sweep the dust behind the door.°

365 *told* counted, tolled   369 *palpable-gross* obviously grotesque
376 *fordone* worn out   377 *wasted* used-up   386 *triple Hecate's
team* i.e., because she had three names: Phoebe in Heaven, Diana
on Earth, Hecate in Hades. (Like her chariot—drawn by black
horses or dragons—the elves were abroad only at night; but
III.ii.388–91 says differently)   389 *frolic* frolicsome   392 *behind
the door* i.e., from behind the door (Puck traditionally helped with
household chores)

Enter King and Queen of Fairies with all their train.

Oberon. Through the house give glimmering light,
   By the dead and drowsy fire:
  Every elf and fairy sprite   395
   Hop as light as bird from brier;
  And this ditty, after me,
  Sing, and dance it trippingly.

Titania. First, rehearse your song by rote,
  To each word a warbling note: 400
  Hand in hand, with fairy grace,
  Will we sing, and bless this place.

                    [Song and dance.]

Oberon. Now, until the break of day,
  Through this house each fairy stray.
  To the best bride-bed will we,   405
  Which by us shall blessèd be;
  And the issue there create°
  Ever shall be fortunate.
  So shall all the couples three
  Ever true in loving be;   410
  And the blots of Nature's hand
  Shall not in their issue stand.
  Never mole, harelip, nor scar,
  Nor mark prodigious,° such as are
  Despisèd in nativity,   415
  Shall upon their children be.
  With this field-dew consecrate,
  Every fairy take his gait,°
  And each several° chamber bless,
  Through this palace, with sweet peace,   420
  And the owner of it blest
  Ever shall in safety rest.
  Trip away; make no stay;
  Meet me all by break of day.

                  Exeunt [all but Puck].

---

407 *create* created   414 *mark prodigious* ominous birthmark   418
take his gait proceed   419 *several* individual

425 *Puck.* If we shadows have offended,
    Think but this, and all is mended:
    That you have but slumb'red here,
    While these visions did appear.
    And this weak and idle° theme,
430   No more yielding but° a dream,
    Gentles, do not reprehend:
    If you pardon, we will mend.
    And, as I am an honest Puck,
    If we have unearnèd luck
435   Now to scape the serpent's tongue,°
    We will make amends ere long;
    Else the Puck a liar call:
    So, good night unto you all.
    Give me your hands,° if we be friends,
440   And Robin shall restore amends.°   [*Exit.*]

FINIS

---

429 *idle* foolish   **430** *No more yielding but* yielding no more than
435 *to scape the serpent's tongue* i.e., to escape hisses from the
audience   **439** *Give me your hands* applaud   **440** *restore amends*
make amends

Textual Note

Our chief authority for the text of *A Midsummer Night's Dream* is the First Quarto of 1600 (Q1), possibly printed from Shakespeare's own manuscript. The Second Quarto of 1619 (Q2), fraudulently dated 1600, and the First Folio of 1623 (F) correct a few obvious mistakes of Q1 and add some new ones. The Folio introduces division into acts. The present text follows Q1 as closely as possible, but modernizes punctuation and spelling (and prints "and" as "an" when it means "if"), occasionally alters the lineation (e.g., prints as prose some lines that were mistakenly set as verse), expands and regularizes the speech prefixes, slightly alters the position of stage directions where necessary, and corrects obvious typographical errors. Other departures from Q1 are listed below, the adopted reading first in italics, and then Q1's reading in roman. If the adopted reading is derived from Q2 or from F, the fact is noted in a bracket following the reading.

I.i.4 *wanes* [Q2] waues 10 *New-bent* Now bent 19 s.d. *Lysander* [F] Lysander and Helena 24 *Stand forth, Demetrius* [printed as s.d. in Q1, Q2, F] 26 *Stand forth, Lysander* [printed as s.d. in Q1, Q2, F] 102 *Demetrius'* Demetrius 136 *low* loue 187 *Yours would* Your words 191 *I'd* ile 216 *sweet* sweld 219 *stranger companies* strange companions

II.i.69 *steep* [Q2] steppe 79 *Aegles* Eagles 109 *thin* chinne 158 *the west* [F] west 190 *slay . . . slayeth* stay . . . stayeth 201 *not nor* [F] not not

II.ii.9, 13, 24 [speech prefixes added by editor]   39 *Be't* Bet it   47 *is*
[Q2] it

III.i.13 *By'r lakin* Berlakin   29–30 *yourselves* [F] your selfe   56
Bottom [Q2] Cet   70 *and let* or let   84 *Odors, odors* [F] odours,
odorous   89 *Puck* [F] Quin   164 *Peaseblossom . . . All* [Q1, Q2,
and F print as a single speech, attributed to "Fairies"]   176 *Peaseblossom . . . Mustardseed. Hail* [Q1, Q2, and F print thus: 1 Fai.
Haile mortall, haile./2. Fai. Haile./3. Fai. Haile]   195 *you of* you

III.ii.19 *mimic* [F] Minnick   80 *part I so* part I   85 *sleep* slippe
213 *first, like* first life   220 *passionate words* [F] words   250
prayers praise   299 *gentlemen* [Q2] gentleman   323 *she's* [Q2] she
is   406 *Speak! In some bush?* Speake in some bush   426 *shalt* [Q2]
shat   451 *To your eye* your eye

IV.i.76 *o'er* or   85 *sleep of all these five* sleepe: of all these, fine
120 *seemed* seeme   131 *this is my* [Q2] this my   175 *saw* see   202
let us [Q2] lets   210 *to expound* [Q2] expound   213 *a patched* [F]
patcht a

IV.ii.3 *Starveling* [F] Flute

V.i.34 *our* [F] or   156 *Snout* [F] Flute   191 *up in thee* [F] now
againe   275 *gleams* beams   320 *mote* moth   353 *Bottom* [F] Lion
373 *lion* Lyons   374 *behowls* beholds   421–22 *And the owner . . .
rest* [these two lines are transposed in Q1, Q2, and F]

A Note on the Source of "A Midsummer Night's Dream"

A Midsummer Night's Dream is, together with *Love's Labor's Lost* and *The Tempest,* one of those few plays for which no specific source appears to exist. The plot, with its skillful interplay of four different actions, is of Shakespeare's own making, although single incidents and motives as well as some names and details come from widely different origins.

Thus, the enveloping action of Theseus and Hippolyta derives in part from Chaucer's *The Knight's Tale.* This tale begins, as our play does, with Theseus' victorious return from war with Hippolyta and also ends with a celebration at court. Moreover, the story of Palamon and Arcite in *The Knight's Tale* is linked with the Theseus story in a similar way and also illustrates how friendship is broken by love. But Shakespeare has modified this motif in a characteristic way, replacing the two men by two young women and adding a fourth lover, thereby not only establishing symmetry but also providing for those multiple combinations and varying relationships between Lysander, Hermia, Demetrius, and Helena that constitute the *comedy of errors* of the night in the forest. Shakespeare's portrait of Theseus may have been further influenced by the figure of Theseus in Plutarch's *Lives,* which Shakespeare read in Sir Thomas North's translation. Theseus' function as a wise judge as well as his tolerance and benevolence toward the craftsmen are features that find a parallel in Plutarch.

Oberon as the fairy king with a kingdom in the East

had been made familiar through the French romance *Huon of Bordeaux,* while the name of Titania for the fairy queen in *A Midsummer Night's Dream* may have been suggested by the epithet given to Diana in Ovid's *Metamorphoses* (III,173). Diana, however, occurs as the "lady of the fairies" in Reginald Scot's *The Discoverie of Witchcraft* (1584), which supplied Shakespeare with much information about witches, fairies, and transformations and contends at the same time that belief in Robin Goodfellow was declining, and that all those stories about fairies were untrue. Bottom's "assification" may also have been suggested by Scot's account of the spells exercised by the witches but has another parallel in Apuleius' *The Golden Ass,* which had been translated in 1566. For the magic juice, several analogues have been pointed out, the closest being in Montemayor's prose pastoral *Diana Enamorada* (1542).

The story of Pyramus and Thisbe existed in Elizabethan times in many poetical versions, some of them exhibiting those sentimental and melodramatic exaggerations that must have prompted Shakespeare to his subtle and complex parody. It is significant that George Pettie in his *Petite Pallace of Pettie his Pleasure* (1576) sees in this story a parallel with the account of *Romeo and Juliet.* Shakespeare in his "play within the play" obviously creates an ironic and comic parallel to his own tragedy—no matter whether *Romeo and Juliet* was already in existence then or soon to appear. Geoffrey Bullough, in the second volume of his *Narrative and Dramatic Sources of Shakespeare,* reprints eleven pieces from which Shakespeare may have drawn.

The most interesting of our play's sources are, however, the unwritten ones. For the fairy world that is presented by so many graphic details and concrete features owes much to folklore and the living tradition of the Warwickshire countryside. Shakespeare must have been intensely alive to the mass of popular superstition, legend, and folk custom still to be found in his own times. He took what he could use from these sources, adding, however, many details of his own invention and modifying several traditional traits. The fairy world which thus emerges is—if we consider its dramatic function—a new creation of Shakespeare's own poetic imagination, which has at each stage transmuted the source material "into something rich and strange."

Commentaries

WILLIAM HAZLITT

from *The Characters of Shakespear's Plays*

Bottom the Weaver is a character that has not had justice done him. He is the most romantic of mechanics. And what a list of companions he has—Quince the Carpenter, Snug the Joiner, Flute the Bellows Mender, Snout the Tinker, Starveling the Tailor; and then again, what a group of fairy attendants, Puck, Peaseblossom, Cobweb, Moth, and Mustardseed! It has been observed that Shakespear's characters are constructed upon deep physiological principles; and there is something in this play which looks very like it. Bottom the Weaver, who takes the lead of

> This crew of patches, rude mechanicals,
> That work for bread upon Athenian stalls,

follows a sedentary trade, and he is accordingly represented as conceited, serious, and fantastical. He is ready to undertake anything and everything, as if it was as much a matter of course as the motion of his loom and shuttle.

From *The Characters of Shakespear's Plays* by William Hazlitt. 2nd ed. London: Taylor & Hessey, 1818.

He is for playing the tyrant, the lover, the lady, the lion. "He will roar that it shall do any man's heart good to hear him"; and this being objected to as improper, he still has a resource in his good opinion of himself, and "will roar you an 'twere any nightingale." Snug the Joiner is the moral man of the piece, who proceeds by measurement and discretion in all things. You see him with his rule and compasses in his hand. "Have you the lion's part written? Pray you, if it be, give it me, for I am slow of study." —"You may do it extempore,"says Quince, "for it is nothing but roaring." Starveling the Tailor keeps the peace, and objects to the lion and the drawn sword. "I believe we must leave the killing out when all's done." Starveling, however, does not start the objections himself, but seconds them when made by others, as if he had not spirit to express his fears without encouragement. It is too much to suppose all this intentional: but it very luckily falls out so. Nature includes all that is implied in the most subtle analytical distinctions; and the same distinctions will be found in Shakespear. Bottom, who is not only chief actor, but stage manager for the occasion, has a device to obviate the danger of frightening the ladies: "Write me a prologue, and let the prologue seem to say, we will do no harm with our swords, and that Pyramus is not killed indeed; and for better assurance, tell them that I, Pyramus, am not Pyramus, but Bottom the Weaver: this will put them out of fear." Bottom seems to have understood the subject of dramatic illusion at least as well as any modern essayist. If our holiday mechanic rules the roost among his fellows, he is no less at home in his new character of an ass, "with amiable cheeks, and fair large ears." He instinctively acquires a most learned taste, and grows fastidious in the choice of dried peas and bottled hay. He is quite familiar with his new attendants, and assigns them their parts with all due gravity. "Monsieur Cobweb, good Monsieur, get your weapon in your hand, and kill me a red-hipt humblebee on the top of a thistle, and, good Monsieur, bring me the honey bag." What an exact knowledge is here shown of natural history!

Puck, or Robin Goodfellow, is the leader of the fairy band. He is the Ariel of the *Midsummer Night's Dream*; and yet as unlike as can be to the Ariel in *The Tempest*. No other poet could have made two such different characters out of the same fanciful materials and situations. Ariel is a minister of retribution, who is touched with the sense of pity at the woes he inflicts. Puck is a madcap sprite, full of wantonness and mischief, who laughs at those whom he misleads—"Lord, what fools these mortals be!" Ariel cleaves the air, and executes his mission with the zeal of a winged messenger; Puck is borne along on his fairy errand like the light and glittering gossamer before the breeze. He is, indeed, a most Epicurean little gentleman, dealing in quaint devices, and faring in dainty delights. Prospero and his world of spirits are a set of moralists: but with Oberon and his fairies we are launched at once into the empire of the butterflies. How beautifully is this race of beings contrasted with the men and women actors in the scene, by a single epithet which Titania gives to the latter, "the human mortals!" It is astonishing that Shakespear should be considered, not only by foreigners, but by many of our own critics, as a gloomy and heavy writer, who painted nothing but "gorgons and hydras, and chimeras dire." His subtlety exceeds that of all other dramatic writers, insomuch that a celebrated person of the present day said that he regarded him rather as a metaphysician than a poet. His delicacy and sportive gaiety are infinite. In the *Midsummer Night's Dream* alone, we should imagine, there is more sweetness and beauty of description than in the whole range of French poetry put together. What we mean is this, that we will produce out of that single play ten passages, to which we do not think any ten passages in the works of the French poets can be opposed, displaying equal fancy and imagery. Shall we mention the remonstrance of Helena to Hermia, or Titania's description of her fairy train, or her disputes with Oberon about the Indian boy, or Puck's account of himself and his employments, or the Fairy Queen's exhortation to the elves to pay due attendance upon her favorite, Bottom; or Hippolita's description of a chase, or Theseus's answer? The two last are as heroical and spirited as the others are full of luscious tenderness. The reading of this play is like wandering in a grove by moonlight: the descriptions breathe a sweetness like odors thrown from beds of flowers.

Titania's exhortation to the fairies to wait upon Bottom, which is remarkable for a certain cloying sweetness in the repetition of the rhymes, is as follows:

> Be kind and courteous to this gentleman.
> Hop in his walks, and gambol in his eyes,
> Feed him with apricocks and dewberries,
> With purple grapes, green figs and mulberries;
> The honey bags steal from the humblebees,
> And for night tapers crop their waxen thighs,
> And light them at the fiery glowworm's eyes,
> To have my love to bed, and to arise:
> And pluck the wings from painted butterflies,
> To fan the moonbeams from his sleeping eyes;
> Nod to him, elves, and do him courtesies.

The sounds of the lute and of the trumpet are not more distinct than the poetry of the foregoing passage, and of the conversation between Theseus and Hippolita.

Theseus. Go, one of you, find out the forester,
> For now our observation is perform'd;
> And since we have the vaward of the day,
> My love shall hear the music of my hounds.
> Uncouple in the western valley, go,
> Dispatch, I say, and find the forester.
> We will, fair Queen, up to the mountain's top,
> And mark the musical confusion
> Of hounds and echo in conjunction.

Hippolyta. I was with Hercules and Cadmus once,
> When in a wood of Crete they bay'd the bear
> With hounds of Sparta; never did I hear
> Such gallant chiding. For besides the groves,
> The skies, the fountains, every region near
> Seem'd all one mutual cry. I never heard
> So musical a discord, such sweet thunder.

Theseus. My hounds are bred out of the Spartan kind,
  So flew'd, so sanded, and their heads are hung
  With ears that sweep away the morning dew;
  Crook-knee'd and dew-lap'd, like Thessalian bulls.
  Slow in pursuit, but matched in mouth like bells,
  Each under each. A cry more tunable
  Was never halloo'd to, nor cheer'd with horn,
  In Crete, in Sparta, nor in Thessaly:
  Judge when you hear.

Even Titian never made a hunting piece of a *gusto* so fresh and lusty, and so near the first ages of the world as this.

It had been suggested to us, that the *Midsummer Night's Dream* would do admirably to get up as a Christmas afterpiece; and our prompter proposed that Mr. Kean should play the part of Bottom, as worthy of his great talents. He might, in the discharge of his duty, offer to play the lady like any of our actresses that he pleased, the lover or the tyrant like any of our actors that he pleased, and the lion like "the most fearful wildfowl living." The carpenter, the tailor, and joiner, it was thought, would hit the galleries. The young ladies in love would interest the side boxes; and Robin Goodfellow and his companions excite a lively fellow feeling in the children from school. There would be two courts, an empire within an empire, the Athenian and the Fairy King and Queen, with their attendants, and with all their finery. What an opportunity for processions, for the sound of trumpets and glittering of spears! What a fluttering of urchins' painted wings; what a delightful profusion of gauze clouds and airy spirits floating on them!

Alas the experiment has been tried, and has failed; not through the fault of Mr. Kean, who did not play the part of Bottom, nor of Mr. Liston, who did, and who played it well, but from the nature of things. The *Midsummer Night's Dream,* when acted, is converted from a delightful fiction into a dull pantomime. All that is finest in the play is lost in the representation. The spectacle was grand: but the spirit was evaporated, the genius was fled.

Poetry and the stage do not agree well together. The attempt to reconcile them in this instance fails not only of effect, but of decorum. The *ideal* can have no place upon the stage, which is a picture without perspective; everything there is in the foreground. That which was merely an airy shape, a dream, a passing thought, immediately becomes an unmanageable reality. Where all is left to the imagination (as is the case in reading) every circumstance, near or remote, has an equal chance of being kept in mind, and tells according to the mixed impression of all that has been suggested. But the imagination cannot sufficiently qualify the actual impressions of the senses. Any offense given to the eye is not to be got rid of by explanation. Thus Bottom's head in the play is a fantastic illusion, produced by magic spells: on the stage it is an ass's head, and nothing more; certainly a very strange costume for a gentleman to appear in. Fancy cannot be embodied any more than a simile can be painted; and it is as idle to attempt it as to personate *Wall* or *Moonshine*. Fairies are not incredible, but fairies six feet high are so. Monsters are not shocking, if they are seen at a proper distance. When ghosts appear at midday, when apparitions stalk along Cheapside, then may the *Midsummer Night's Dream* be represented without injury at Covent Garden or at Drury Lane. The boards of a theater and the regions of fancy are not the same thing.

EDWARD DOWDEN

from *Shakspere: A Critical Study of His Mind and Art*

The play was perhaps so named because it is a dream play, the fantastic adventures of a night, and because it was first represented in midsummer—the midsummer, perhaps, of 1594. The imagined season of the action of the play is the beginning of May, for, according to the magnificent piece of medieval-classical mythology embodied here, and in the *Knightes Tale* of Chaucer, and again in the *Two Noble Kinsmen* of Shakspere and Fletcher, this was the month of Theseus's marriage with his Amazonian bride.[1] In like manner, the play of *Twelfth Night* received its name probably because it was first enacted at that season of festivity; and as if to declare more emphatically that it shall be nameless, Shakspere adds a second title, *Twelfth Night, or What You Will;* that is (for we need seek no deeper significance), *Twelfth Night,* or anything you like to call it. *A Midsummer Night's Dream* was written on the occasion of the marriage of some noble couple—possibly for the marriage of the poet's patron Southampton with Elizabeth Vernon, as Mr. Gerald Massey supposes; possibly at an earlier

From *Shakspere: A Critical Study of His Mind and Art* by Edward Dowden. 3rd ed., 1877. Reprinted by permission of Routledge & Kegan Paul Ltd.

[1] Titania says to Oberon (Act II, Scene i):
  And never since the middle summer's spring
  Met we on hill, in dale, forest, or mead, etc.
Perhaps a night in early May might be considered a night in the spring of midsummer.

date, to do honor to the marriage of the Earl of Essex with Lady Sidney.[2]

The central figure of the play is that of Theseus. There is no figure in the early drama of Shakspere so magnificent. His are the large hands that have helped to shape the world. His utterance is the rich-toned speech of one who is master of events—who has never known a shrill or eager feeling. His nuptial day is at hand; and while the other lovers are agitated, bewildered, incensed, Theseus, who does not think of himself as a lover, but rather as a beneficent conqueror, remains in calm possession of his joy. Theseus, a grand ideal figure, is to be studied as Shakspere's conception of the heroic man of action in his hour of enjoyment and of leisure. With a splendid capacity for enjoyment, gracious to all, ennobled by the glory, implied rather than explicit, of great foregone achievement, he stands as center of the poem, giving their true proportions to the fairy tribe, upon the one hand, and, upon the other, to the "human mortals." The heroic men of action—Theseus, Henry V, Hector— are supremely admired by Shakspere. Yet it is observable that as the total Shakspere is superior to Romeo, the man given over to passion, and to Hamlet, the man given over to thought, so the Hamlet and the Romeo within him give Shakspere an infinite advantage over even the most heroic men of action. He admires these men of action supremely, but he admires them from an outside point of

2 Mr. Massey is obliged to entertain the supposition that the play was written some time before the marriage actually took place (1598), "at a period when it may have been thought the Queen's consent could be obtained. . . . I have ventured the date of 1595" (*Shakespeare's Sonnets and His Private Friends,* p. 481). Professor Karl Elze's theory, maintained in a highly ingenious paper in *Shakespeare-Jahrbuch,* Vol. III, that the play was written for the marriage of the young Earl of Essex, would throw back the date to 1590—a good deal too early, I believe. Professor Elze has, however, much to say in favor of this opinion. See also the excellent article by Hermann Kurz in *Shakespeare-Jahrbuch,* Vol. IV. Illustrations of the Fairy Mythology of *A Midsummer Night's Dream* will be found in the volume by Halliwell bearing that name, issued by the Shakespeare Society (1845), and also in *Shakspere-Forschungen,* II, "Nachklänge germanischer Mythe," by Benno Tschischwitz (1868). Mr. Halpin's exceedingly ingenious study of Oberon's Vision interprets that celebrated passage as having reference to Leicester's intrigue with Lettice, daughter of Sir Francis Knollys, and wife of Walter Devereux, Earl of Essex.

view. "These fellows of infinite tongue," says Henry, wooing the French princess, "that can rhyme themselves into ladies' favors, they do always reason themselves out again. What! a speaker is but a prater, a rhyme is but a ballad." It is into Theseus's mouth that Shakspere puts the words which class together "the lunatic, the lover, and the poet" as of imagination all compact. That is the touch which shows how Shakspere stood off from Theseus, did not identify himself with this grand ideal (which he admired so truly), and admitted to himself a secret superiority of his own soul over that of this noble master of the world.

Comments by Shakspere upon his own art are not so numerous that we can afford to overlook them. It must here be noted that Shakspere makes the "palpable gross" interlude of the Athenian mechanicals serve as an indirect apology for his own necessarily imperfect attempt to represent fairy land and the majestic world of heroic life. Maginn writes, "When Hippolyta speaks scornfully of the tragedy in which Bottom holds so conspicuous a part, Theseus answers that the best of this kind [scenic performances] are but shadows, and the worst no worse if imagination amend them. She answers [for Hippolyta has none of Theseus's indulgence towards inefficiency, but rather a woman's intolerance of the absurd] that it must be *your* imagination then, not *theirs*. He retorts with a joke on the vanity of actors, and the conversation is immediately changed. The meaning of the Duke is that however we may laugh at the silliness of Bottom and his companions in their ridiculous play, the author labors under no more than the common calamity of dramatists. They are all but dealers in shadowy representations of life; and if the worst among them can set the mind of the spectator at work, he is equal to the best."[3]

Maginn has missed the more important significance of the passage. Its dramatic appropriateness is the essential point to observe. To Theseus, the great man of action, the worst and the best of these shadowy representations

3 *Shakspeare Papers*, p. 119.

are all one. He graciously lends himself to be amused, and will not give unmannerly rebuff to the painstaking craftsmen who have so laboriously done their best to please him. But Shakspere's mind by no means goes along with the utterance of Theseus in this instance any more than when he places in a single group the lover, the lunatic, and the poet. With one principle enounced by the Duke, however, Shakspere evidently does agree— namely, that it is the business of the dramatist to set the spectator's imagination to work; that the dramatist must rather appeal to the mind's eye than to the eye of sense; and that the cooperation of the spectator with the poet is necessary. For the method of Bottom and his company is precisely the reverse, as Gervinus has observed, of Shakspere's own method. They are determined to leave nothing to be supplied by the imagination. Wall must be plastered; Moonshine must carry lantern and bush. And when Hippolyta, again becoming impatient of absurdity, exclaims, "I am aweary of this moon! would he would change!" Shakspere further insists on his piece of dramatic criticism by urging, through the Duke's mouth, the absolute necessity of the man in the moon being *within* his lantern. Shakspere as much as says, "If you do not approve my dramatic method of presenting fairy land and the heroic world, here is a specimen of the rival method. You think my fairy world might be amended. Well, amend it with your own imagination. I can do no more unless I adopt the artistic ideas of these Athenian handicraftsmen."[4]

It is a delightful example of Shakspere's impartiality that he can represent Theseus with so much genuine enthusiasm. Mr. Matthew Arnold has named our aristocrats, with their hardy, efficient manners, their addiction to field sports, and their hatred of ideas, "the Barbarians." Theseus is a splendid and gracious aristocrat, perhaps not without a touch of the Barbarian in him. He would have

4 On Shakspere's studies of chivalric medieval poetry, see some interesting pages in Mr. Spalding's *Letter on Shakspere's Authorship of the* "Two Noble Kinsmen," pp. 67–75 the article "Chaucer and Shakspere" in the *Quarterly Review,* Jan., 1873; and Hertzberg's learned discussion of the sources of the Troilus story in *Shakespeare-Jahrbuch,* Vol. VI.

found Hamlet a wholly unintelligible person, who, in possession of his own thoughts, could be contented in a nutshell. When Shakspere wrote *The Two Gentlemen of Verona,* in which, with little dramatic propriety, the Duke of Milan celebrates "the force of heaven-bred poesy," we may reasonably suppose that the poet might not have been quite just to one who was indifferent to art. But now his self-mastery has increased, and therefore with unfeigned satisfaction he presents Theseus, the master of the world, who, having beauty and heroic strength in actual possession, does not need to summon them to occupy his imagination—the great chieftain to whom art is a very small concern of life, fit for a leisure hour between battle and battle. Theseus, who has nothing antique or Grecian about him, is an idealized study from the life. Perhaps he is idealized Essex, perhaps idealized Southampton. Perhaps some night a dramatic company was ordered to perform in presence of a great Elizabethan noble—we know not whom—who needed to entertain his guests, and there, in a moment of fine imaginative vision, the poet discovered Theseus.

ENID WELSFORD

from *The Court Masque*

For the question as to the relation between *A Midsummer Night's Dream, The Tempest,* and the court masque, is not merely a matter of classification: behind it lies the vital question as to how far the art of a nation is dependent on the quantity and quality of its recreation, and how far the individual genius is dependent upon the artistic talent diffused throughout society.

The suggestion that *A Midsummer Night's Dream* and *The Tempest* should be regarded as masques has little to recommend it. In all probability both plays were written for the celebration of court weddings, but they are not masques, because there are no masquers, because they are independent of their occasion, because their plots are not mere inductions leading up to masque dances, because there is nothing in them corresponding to the sudden failure of detachment which occurs at the end of Peele's *Arraignment of Paris,* and even to a lesser extent in the final scene of Milton's *Comus.* On the other hand, if they are further removed from the masque form, they are much closer to its spirit than is *Comus.* For Shakespeare perceived, or at any rate acted upon, the principle that the masque must die to live. Ben Jonson failed nobly in his effort to exalt the soul of the masque, because he was

From *The Court Masque* by Enid Welsford. Cambridge: Cambridge University Press; New York: The Macmillan Company, 1927. Reprinted by permission of Cambridge University Press.

forever hampered by its body, but Shakespeare, being a playwright, not a masque poet, was able to disregard the masque body altogether, and instead of having to supply the place of music, carpentry, and dancing by inadequate prose description, he transmuted all these things into poetry, and wove them into the very texture of his plays.

The scenic element is almost as important in *A Midsummer Night's Dream* as in the masque, but it is treated in a very different way. The wood near Athens is not dependent upon, rather it is antagonistic to, the art of the scene painter. Even if *A Midsummer Night's Dream* was well staged at court, still Oberon's description of his surrounding could hardly be translated into terms of paint and canvas, for what scene painter would be quite equal to the "bank where the wild thyme blows," or, indeed, what human actor could obey Titania's stage direction:

> Come, now a roundel and a fairy song;
> Then, for the third part of a minute, hence?

The feeling of the countryside, the romantic fairy-haunted earth has affected the very details of language.

> Your eyes are lodestars; and your tongue's sweet air
> More tunable than lark to shepherd's ear,
> When wheat is green, when hawthorn buds appear.

When Bottom appears with his ass's head:

> As wild geese that the creeping fowler eye,
> Or russet-pated choughs, many in sort,
> Rising and cawing at the gun's report,
> Sever themselves and madly sweep the sky;
> So, at his sight, away his fellows fly.

Titania winds Bottom in her arms:

> So doth the woodbine the sweet honeysuckle
> Gently entwist; the female ivy so
> Enrings the barky fingers of the elm.

"Acorn," "canker blossom," "hindering knot grass," are epithets flung at each other by the quarrelsome lovers.

When Duke Theseus has left the lovers to themselves, Demetrius, still dazed and only half awake, murmurs:

> These things seem small and undistinguishable,
> Like far-off mountains turned into clouds.

It is a fine image, giving just that suggestion of awe and uncertainty which was needed to soften the transition from dream to waking life. The magic of the phrase lies in the words "small" and "undistinguishable." A lesser poet would probably have given the abstract idea in the first line and in the second its concrete illustration. But the word "small" (instead of "strange," "vague" or some other word of that kind) at once sets the imagination to work and suggests the picture which the next line expands, and the sound of the word "undistinguishable," with its accumulated syllables trailing off into silence, does for the ear what the word "small" does for the eye, suggests the shimmering atmosphere, the blurred outline, and the gradual vanishing of the distant mountains on the horizon.

Shakespeare has absorbed the scenic splendor of the masque, not only in description and picturesque language, but also in a blending of tones, a harmony of colors, which the poet has attained by a most delicate and subtle handling of the laws of resemblance and contrast. The play opens in the daylight, first in the court, then in the cottage, and brings us into the presence of the two sets of characters who most emphatically belong to daylight and the solid earth, the genial cultivated rulers, the simple-minded artisans, the former serving as a framework, the latter as a foil to the poetry and moonshine of the dream. The excellence of the workmanship lies in the fact that the framework is organically connected with the picture, for Theseus and Hippolyta are accompanied by Philostrate the Master of the Revels. We are in the world of men, but men are in holiday mood. Ordinary workaday business is set aside, pomp, triumph, and reveling are in

the air. Anything may happen. The moon is at once made
the topic of conversation:

> Four days will quickly steep themselves in night;
> Four nights will quickly dream away the time;
> And then the moon, like to a silver bow
> New-bent in heaven, shall behold the night
> Of our solemnities.

By the end of the first act our minds are full of the wood
where Helena and Hermia used to lie "upon faint primrose beds," where the young people used to meet "to do
observance to a morn of May," and where very shortly
lovers and workmen are to assemble by moonlight for
diverse purposes. Moonshine is almost as real a personage
in Shakespeare's as in Bottom's play. Her presence per-
meates the action, a delicate compliment to the maiden
Queen, and Titania is merely a glancing beam of her
light. Even the workmen help to make her presence felt:

Quince. Well, it shall be so. But there is two hard things, that is,
to bring the moonlight into a chamber; for, you know,
Pyramus and Thisby meet by moonlight.

Snout. Doth the moon shine that night we play our play?

Bottom. A calendar, a calendar! look in the almanac; find out
moonshine, find out moonshine.

Quince. Yes, it doth shine that night.

Bottom. Why, then may you leave a casement of the great
chamber window, where we play, open; and the moon may
shine in at the casement.

Quince. Ay; or else one must come in with a bush of thorns
and a lanthorne and say he comes to disfigure, or to present,
the person of Moonshine.

But if the transition from daylight to moonlight is delicately wrought; it is far surpassed by the gradual oncom-
ing of the dawn in Acts III and IV.

The first hint comes when Oberon commands Puck to
cover the starry welkin with fog, the better to mislead the
angry lovers. The latter replies:

My fairy lord, this must be done with haste,
For night's swift dragons cut the clouds full fast,
And yonder shines Aurora's harbinger.

Then in comes Lysander vainly hunting for Demetrius.
Thwarted by the darkness, he lies down to rest:

Come, thou gentle day!
For if but once thou show me thy gray light,
I'll find Demetrius and revenge this spite.

In comes Demetrius in similar mood:

Thou shalt buy this dear,
If ever I thy face by daylight see:
Now, go thy way. Faintness constraineth me
To measure out my length on this cold bed:
By day's approach look to be visited.

But the women are suffering even more than the men
from that exhaustion and bedraggledness, which is so
oppressive in the small hours after a sleepless night:

Re-enter Helena.

Helena. O weary night! O long and tedious night,
Abate thy hours! Shine, comforts, from the east!
That I may back to Athens by daylight. . . .

Re-enter Hermia.

Hermia. Never so weary, never so in woe,
Bedabbled with the dew and torn with briers,
I can no further crawl, no further go;
My legs can keep no pace with my desires.
Here will I rest me till the break of day.
Heavens shield Lysander, if they mean a fray!

The lovers are all asleep on the flowery bank, when they
are joined by Titania, Bottom, and the fairies. Bottom
has "an exposition of sleep" come upon him and, as he

and the Fairy Queen rest together, Oberon and Puck arrive and conquer Cupid's flower by Dian's bud. Titania wakes, freed from the spell, takes hands with Oberon, and the day dawns.

Puck. Fairy King, attend, and mark:
  I do hear the morning lark.

Oberon. Then, my Queen, in silence sad,
  Trip we after the night's shade;
  We the globe can compass soon,
  Swifter than the wandering moon.

The fairies vanish, a horn winds, Theseus, Hippolyta, and the rest break in with a clatter of horses and hounds, the day breaks, and the shadows flee away. But the broad sunlight is not suited to the Midsummer Night's Dream, the day soon passes and gives place to torchlight. It would have been a simple plan to leave the fairy part in the center of the play as a dream interval in the waking workaday world, but Shakespeare knew better than that. There is nothing more disappointing to a child than to find that the fairy tale was only a dream after all, and children know best how a fairy tale should be conducted.

The iron tongue of midnight hath tolled twelve;
Lovers, to bed; 'tis almost fairy time.

Once more the coloring changes. The mortals are gone, the bright festal lights are dimmed, "now the wasted brands do glow," now the fire is dead and drowsy, and very quietly, very lightly, the fairies come in; dreamland has invaded reality, and who shall say which is which, for Puck left behind with his broom and his parting word sweeps the whole thing away, like the leaves of yesteryear.

To compare a very great with a very small thing, the imaginative effect of this kind of plot weaving is like that of the transformation scenes in ballet or pantomime, where groups of dancers come in like waves of color, melting one into another. The effect is attractive even when crudely and unbeautifully designed. Transmuted into poetry, it is of surpassing charm. It could only have been so transmuted at a time when pageantry was part of the people's life, when beauty was an element in all their recreations and "they drew it in as simply as their breath."

Music in the court masque was even more important than scenery. Again and again, in the accounts of Elizabethan and Jacobean revels, we are told of the entrancing quality of the music. Robert Laneham told his merchant friend how Elizabeth stood by night on the bridge at Kenilworth and listened to the music sounding from barges on the quiet water. The music which accompanied the show of the *Lady of the Lake* moved him to ecstasy:

> Noow, Syr, the ditty in mitter so aptly endighted to the matter, and after by voys so deliciously deliver'd . . . every instrument agayn in hiz kind so excellently tunabl; and this in the eeving of the day, resoounding from the calm waters, whear prezens of her Majesty, and longing to listen, had utterly damped all noyz and dyn; the hole armony conveyd in tyme, tune, and temper thus incomparably melodious; with what pleazure, Master Martyn, with what sharpnes of conceyt, with what lyvely delighte, this moought pears [pierce] into the heerers harts; I pray ye imagin yoorself az ye may; for, so God judge me, by all the wit and cunning I have, I cannot express, I promis yoo. . . . Muzik iz a nobl art![1]

This music Shakespeare has transmuted into his poetry, as he has transmuted the spectacular element of pageantry. Laneham's emotion still vibrates in the words of Oberon:

> My gentle Puck, come hither. Thou remember'st
> Since once I sat upon a promontory,
> And heard a mermaid on a dolphin's back
> Uttering such dulcet and harmonious breath,
> That the rude sea grew civil at her song,

[1] Laneham's *Account of the Queen's Entertainment at Killingworth Castle*, 1575, reprinted in *Prog. Eliz.* Vol. 1, pp. 458, 459.

And certain stars shot madly from their spheres,
To hear the sea maid's music.

The whole play is musically written. It is interesting to
compare Milton's famous "Sabrina" lyric with any of the
fairy songs in *A Midsummer Night's Dream* and *The
Tempest*. In "Sabrina" each word is exquisitely right, each
word is an entity with its own peculiar value. In Shakespeare's songs the words melt into one another, and sometimes meaning is almost lost in melody and emotion.
There is the same musical quality in the flowing blank
verse of *A Midsummer Night's Dream*, verse which is lyrical rather than dramatic; liquid clear, never checked in its
course by some sudden, sharp, projecting thought. Milton's dialogue has the terse, stichomythic quality of
Greek or Senecan drama, Shakespeare's is a part-song.[2]

The real soul of the masque, however, was the rhythmic movement of living bodies. It is owing to this fact that
A Midsummer Night's Dream is more nearly related to
the genuine masque than is *Comus*. In *Comus,* as we
have seen, though dances occur, they are merely inci-
dental, and the play would be scarcely altered by their
omission. In *A Midsummer Night's Dream* most—not
all—of the dances are vitally connected with the plot.
For instance, Titania's awakening in Act IV, Scene i is an
important point in the play, for it is the point where the
ravel begins to be untangled, and the occasion is celebrated by a dance of reunion between Fairy King and
Fairy Queen:

Oberon. Sound, music! Come, my Queen, take hands with me,
And rock the ground whereon these sleepers be.
Now thou and I are new in amity,
And will tomorrow midnight solemnly
Dance in Duke Theseus' house triumphantly,
And bless it to all fair prosperity.
There shall the pairs of faithful lovers be
Wedded, with Theseus, all in jollity.

2 Cf. *A Midsummer Night's Dream*, I.i.132ff., with *Comus*, ll.271ff.

The rhythm of the poetry is a dance rhythm, the lines rock and sway with the movement of the fairies. Even more closely in the last scene does the verse echo the light pattering steps of the elves. There is nothing like this in *Comus*. The lyrics there are exquisite, melodious, but they are not dance songs. Even the entry of Comus is poetry of the *Il penseroso* order, imaginative, intellectual, reminiscent, while Shakespeare's lines are alive with movement, and suggest the repeat and turn and rhythmic beat of dancing. In a word, in *Comus* we have thought turned to poetry, while in *A Midsummer Night's Dream* we have sound and movement turned to poetry.

The influence of the dance has affected not merely isolated songs and speeches, but the whole structure of *A Midsummer Night's Dream*. Again a comparison with *Comus* is helpful. The difference in style between *Comus* and *A Midsummer Night's Dream* depends upon a difference of spirit. *Comus* is a criticism of life, it springs from an abstract idea: *A Midsummer Night's Dream* is a dance, a movement of bodies. The plot is a pattern, a figure, rather than a series of events occasioned by human character and passion, and this pattern, especially in the moonlight parts of the play, is the pattern of a dance.

Enter a Fairie at one doore, and Robin Goodfellow at another. . . . Enter the King of Fairies, at one doore, with his traine; and the Queene, at another with hers.

The appearance and disappearance and reappearance of the various lovers, the will-o'-the-wisp movement of the elusive Puck, form a kind of figured ballet. The lovers quarrel in a dance pattern: first, there are two men to one woman and the other woman alone, then for a brief space a circular movement, each one pursuing and pursued, then a return to the first figure with the position of the women reversed, then a cross-movement, man quarreling with man and woman with woman, and then, as finale, a general setting to partners, including not only lovers but fairies and royal personages as well.

This dancelike structure makes it inevitable that the

lovers should be almost as devoid of character as masquers or masque presenters. The harmony and grace of the action would have been spoiled by convincing passion.

The only character study in *A Midsummer Night's Dream* is to be found in the portrayal of Bottom, Theseus, and perhaps Hippolyta. Even in drawing these characters Shakespeare was evidently influenced by the memory of pageants, complimentary speeches, and entertainments addressed by townspeople and humble folk to the Queen or to the nobility. A glance through Nichols' *Public Progresses* shows what innumerable lengthy speeches, what innumerable disguisings and shows, Elizabeth was obliged to bear with gracious demeanor. Her experiences were similar to those of Theseus:

> Where I have come, great clerks have purposed
> To greet me with premeditated welcomes;
> Where I have seen them shiver and look pale,
> Make periods in the midst of sentences,
> Throttle their practic'd accent in their fears,
> And, in conclusion, dumbly have broke off,
> Not paying me a welcome.

One Sunday afternoon, at Kenilworth Castle, Elizabeth and her court whiled away the time by watching the countrypeople at a Brideale and Morris Dance. Their amused kindly tolerance is just that of Theseus and the lovers towards the Athenian workmen. So that even in the most solid and dramatic parts of his play Shakespeare is only giving an idealized version of courtly and country revels and of the people that played a part in them.

In *A Midsummer Night's Dream* Bottom and his companions serve the same purpose as the antimasque in the courtly revels. It is true that Shakespeare's play was written before Ben Jonson had elaborated and defined the antimasque, but from the first grotesque dances were popular, and the principle of contrast was always latent in the masque. There is, however, a great difference between Jonson's and Shakespeare's management of foil and relief. In the antimasque the transition is sudden and the contrast complete,[3] a method of composition effective enough in spectacle and ballet. But in a play, as Shakespeare well knew, the greatest beauty is gained through contrast when the difference is obvious and striking, but rises out of a deep though unobstrusive resemblance This could not be better illustrated than by the picture of Titania winding the ass-headed Bottom in her arms. Why is it that this is a pleasing picture, why is it that the rude mechanicals do not, as a matter of fact, disturb or sully Titania's "close and consecrated bower"? Malvolio in Bottom's place would be repellent, yet Malvolio, regarded superficially, is less violently contrasted to the Fairy Queen than is Nick Bottom. Bottom with his ass's head is grotesquely hideous, and in ordinary life he is crude, raw, and very stupid. We have no reason to suppose that Malvolio was anything but a well-set-up, proper-looking man, spruce, well dressed, the perfect family butler. His mentality too is of a distinctly higher order than Bottom's. He fills a responsible position with credit, he follows a reasoned line of conduct, he thinks nobly of the soul. Two things alone he lacks (and that is why no self-respecting fay could ever kiss him)—humor and imagination. Malvolio is, therefore, the only character who cannot be included in the final harmony of *Twelfth Night*. Bottom and his fellows did perhaps lack humor (though the interview with the fairies suggests that Bottom had a smack of it), but in its place they possessed unreason. Imagination they did have, of the most simple, primal, childlike kind. It is their artistic ambition that lifts them out of the humdrum world and turns them into Midsummer Dreamers, and we have seen how cunningly Shakespeare extracts from their very stupidity romance and moonshine. But, indeed, grotesqueness and stupidity (of a certain kind) have a kinship with beauty. For these qualities usually imply a measure of spiritual freedom, they lead to at least a temporary relief from the tyranny of reason and from the pressure of the external world. In *A Midsummer Night's Dream* the dominance of the Lord of Misrule is not marked by coarse

[3] Cf. *The Masque of Queens*, and *supra*, pp. 183, 267.

parody, but by the partial repeal of the laws of cause and effect. By delicate beauty, gentle mockery, and simple romantic foolishness our freedom is gained.

If Shakespeare's play had, like *Comus,* been based upon an abstract idea, he might have found in Malvolio, not in Bottom, the most effective contrast to the Fairy Queen. The contrast between the prosaic man of business and the pierrot or elfin type of creature is a recurrent theme in literature. The amusement lies in putting the prosy people in charming or unconventional surroundings and laughing at their inadequacy and confusion—

> Big fat woman whom nobody loves,
> Why do you walk through the fields with gloves,
> Missing so much and so much?

But either gloves or yellow stockings and cross garters would shatter Shakespeare's dream. For his play is not a criticism of life but a dance, and a dance of which the underlying motif is harmony. The contrast may be sharp as you please, but the unity must be deeper than the divergence. For, after all, the presiding deity is Hymen. His functions are performed by the fairies who are, indeed, emanations from him. Deeply rooted in folklore is the connection between the fairies and fertility, and Shakespeare had a happy inspiration when he substituted them for the Ceres, Dianas, and Junos of pageantry, and also turned them into an expression of the harmony and concord which was the keystone of most Elizabethan revels.

HENRY ALONZO MYERS

"Romeo and Juliet" and *"A Midsummer Night's Dream"*: Tragedy and Comedy

At the end of Plato's *Symposium* we find an amusing picture of a great philosopher putting Agathon, the tragic poet, and Aristophanes, the greatest comic poet of Athens, to sleep with his discourse on the nature of tragedy and comedy. As Plato tells the story, it happened in the early hours of the morning, after a night spent in feasting and singing the praises of love:

> There remained [of the company] only Socrates, Aristophanes, and Agathon, who were drinking out of a large goblet which they passed round, and Socrates was discoursing to them. Aristodemus was only half awake, and he did not hear the beginning of the discourse; the chief thing which he remembered was Socrates compelling the other two to acknowledge that the genius of comedy was the same with that of tragedy, and that the true artist in tragedy was an artist in comedy also. To this they were constrained to assent, being drowsy, and not quite following the argument. And first of all Aristophanes dropped

From *Tragedy: A View of Life* by Henry Alonzo Myers. Ithaca, N.Y.: Cornell University Press, 1956. Copyright 1956 by Cornell University Press. Reprinted by permission of the publishers.

off, then, when the day was already dawning, Agathon.
Socrates, having laid them to sleep, rose to depart. [Jow-
ett translation]

Like all good comedy, this scene is entertaining as well
as instructive. It is entertaining because it presents the
opposite of the order we naturally expect: a tragic poet
and a comic poet, whom we expect to be interested in
a discourse on the nature of tragedy and comedy, fall
asleep; it is instructive because it makes the point, evident
elsewhere in literary history, that tragic and comic poets
do not need explicitly formulated theories of tragedy and
comedy, that they are often indifferent to such abstract
speculations.

The distinctive form and significance of tragedies and
comedies indicate, however, that the successful poets
have had an adequate sense of the tragic and the comic.
Apparently the appreciative reader or spectator also possesses this mysterious but adequate sense of the nature
of tragedy and comedy, for as the artist can create without an explicitly formulated theory, so the reader can
appreciate and enjoy the specific work of art without
the benefit of definitions and generalizations. But although speculation about the nature of tragedy and
comedy is not indispensable to either creation or appreciation, it is, nevertheless, a natural and, indeed, inevitable result of our curiosity as rational beings. If it did not
begin before, dramatic theory began as the first spectators
were leaving the first performance in the first theater.
When we have had an intensely interesting experience,
we are eager to know its nature and its causes. Why do
we enjoy the spectacle of a man who falls from prosperity to adversity? Why do we laugh at fools? As long
as we are interested in drama and in its sources in life,
we shall be asking these questions and trying to answer
them.

The assertion that the genius of tragedy is the same
as that of comedy and that the true artist in tragedy is
an artist in comedy also is the kind of provocative conundrum or apparent paradox which Socrates loved to dis-
cuss. It was a bold speculative assertion rather than a

description of known facts, for the Greek dramatic poets, as we know them, kept tragedy and comedy apart and excelled in one or the other, not in both. Plato, who recorded the assertion, supported it in practice by displaying a sharp comic sense in the *Symposium* and a deep tragic sense in the dialogues which describe the trial and death of Socrates. But its support in drama did not come until the 1590's, when Shakespeare wrote *Romeo and Juliet* and *A Midsummer Night's Dream,* displaying genius in both tragedy and comedy.

What did Socrates have in mind? If the genius of tragedy is the same as that of comedy, what is the difference between the two? Certainly, he rejected the popular choice of the distinction between an unhappy and a happy ending as the difference between tragedy and comedy: in Plato's *Philebus* he maintains that we view both forms of drama with mingled pleasure and pain, smiling through our tears at tragedy and responding to the ridiculous in others with laughter, which is pleasant, tinged with envy, which is unpleasant. But this view, although it supports the assertion that tragedy and comedy are similar, leaves us, if both have the same effect, with no way of distinguishing one from the other. It can hardly be all that Socrates had in mind.

After years of wondering what he had in mind when his audience at the symposium failed him, I do not know the answer, but I have reached the point where I know what I should have said if I had been Socrates and if I had been more fortunate than he in holding my audience.

Man, I should have said, is a rational animal: he is always looking for meaning in his experience. He looks for meaning and order everywhere, but since the desire to find some significant pattern in his joys and sorrows, some just relation between good and evil, is closest to his heart, surpassing even his desire to grasp the order of the physical world, he looks most intently for meaning in the realm of values. That is why tragedy, which is an artistic demonstration that justice governs our joys and sorrows, has always seemed to most critics to be the highest form of art.

Since man has only a finite intelligence, he cannot always find the order he craves, either in the inner world of values or in the outer world of science and external description. In his search for order he is everywhere confronted by disorder, absurdity, nonsense, and incongruity. Fortunately, however, he finds in laughter, at least in his relaxed moments, an enjoyable emotional reaction to these disappointments to his reason. We rightly honor the comic poet, who by presenting nonsense in contrast to sense points up the difference between the two and who through laughter reconciles us to those experiences which frustrate the effort of reason to find meaningful patterns in all experience.

Order and disorder, the congruous and the incongruous, sense and nonsense, profundity and absurdity are pairs of opposites; each member of each pair throws light on the other so that whoever has a keen sense of order, congruity, sense, and profundity must also have a keen sense of disorder, incongruity, nonsense, and absurdity. Clearly, then, if the discovery of order in the realm of good and evil is the glory of tragedy, which finds intelligibility and justice in our seemingly chance joys and sorrows, and if the glory of comedy lies in its transformation of the frustrations of reasoning into soothing laughter, the artist in tragedy may also be an artist in comedy, and vice versa; and it may also be said that the genius of tragedy is similar to that of comedy.

Socrates, who was a rationalist, might well have expounded his apparent paradox in this fashion; very probably, however, the rivalry between philosophers and poets in his time would have made it difficult for him to recognize the tragic poets as the discoverers of justice in our joys and sorrows and the comic poets as the teachers of the difference between sense and nonsense. Since we can never know what Socrates had in mind, the final episode of the *Symposium* must remain, as Plato intended, a frustration of reason made pleasant by laughter at the absurdity of the ideal audience falling asleep in the presence of the right speaker on the right subject. This pleasant frustration does not prevent us, however, from determining for ourselves whether the great teacher's provocative conundrum will serve as a key to the meaning of tragedy and comedy.

The hypothesis which I have offered as a substitute for the slumber-stifled discussion needs amplification and verification by specific examples. What better test can be found than the first test afforded by the history of dramatic literature—the appearance of *Romeo and Juliet* and *A Midsummer Night's Dream* as the works of one author? These plays prove that Shakespeare, at least, was an artist in both tragedy and comedy. Do they indicate also that the genius of tragedy is similar to that of comedy? Do they indicate that the two are related as order is related to disorder—that the function of tragedy is to reveal a just order in our joys and sorrows and the function of comedy to turn disorder into soothing laughter?

II

The answers to two questions lead us directly to the heart of the tragic meaning of *Romeo and Juliet*. The first question is, What causes the downfall of the hero and of the heroine who shares his fate? The second question is, In what sense does the play have universality: does the fate of Romeo and Juliet represent the fate of all lovers?

Shakespeare himself could not have correctly answered the first question—What causes the downfall of the hero and heroine?—before he finished the play. *Romeo and Juliet* is Shakespeare's first true tragedy; as he wrote it, he was developing his own sense of the tragic. He started the play with a view which he found unsatisfactory as he went on writing and ended with a view which he upheld in all his later tragedies. He started with the view that something outside the hero is the cause of his downfall, that something outside man is the cause of the individual's particular fate.

His first view is stressed in the Prologue, which announces that "a pair of star-cross'd lovers take their life." This forecast points ahead to Romeo's exclamation, when he hears and believes the report of Juliet's death:

Is it even so? then I defy you, stars!

From this point on, every step he takes leads to his downfall. He buys poison from the apothecary, goes to Juliet's tomb, drinks the poison, and dies—while Juliet still lives. The stars are triumphant. Romeo's defiance of his fate hastens its fulfillment.

The stars are symbolic of the elements of bad luck and chance in the action of the play, of the bad luck which involves Romeo in a renewal of the feud and of the chance delay of the messenger who would have told him that Juliet lived. But do the stars, do chance and bad luck, determine the particular fate of the individual? Bad luck and chance are facts of life, but is there a deeper fact than chance and bad luck, a truer cause of the individual's fate? Like Romeo, we all suffer at times from bad luck. Like Romeo, we all hear rumors and alarms and false warnings and reports of danger and disaster. We know from experience that our response to these chance and unlucky events is more important than the events themselves; and our responses depend upon our characters. Character is a deeper and more important influence in human affairs than luck or chance.

Some time ago a radio program presented, as a remarkable illustration of chance and bad luck, the story of a man from Pennsylvania who had been hit by a train three times at the same crossing. When we reflect upon his story, we are likely to conclude that it is a revelation of character rather than an illustration of chance. If we had been in his place, most of us, after the first accident, would have taken all possible precautionary measures to see that it did not happen again; and if by chance we were struck again by an unscheduled train on a day when the crossing signals were not working, it seems likely that we would never again cross the tracks at that point. It is difficult for us to avoid the conclusion that the man from Pennsylvania was the kind of man who gets hit by trains.

Examples of "chance" and "bad luck" are common in the news. The following is representative of many: "A year to the day after he broke his left leg in a fall caused by a loose plank in his doorstep, John Jones, 47, of . . . , broke his right leg when he tripped over the same plank." Obviously, this is another revelation of character: Jones is the kind of man who will risk another leg rather than fix the plank.

While writing his first tragedy, Shakespeare discovered that the individual's fate is determined from within, by character, and not from without, by chance or bad luck. Although the character of Romeo is not as clearly revealed as the characters of Lear, Hamlet, Macbeth, and Othello, it is nevertheless certain from a point early in the play that Romeo is the kind of person who is inclined to accept bad news at its face value and who is inclined, when he is confronted by apparent disaster, toward some despairing deed. In his despair when the feud broke out— at a time when he knew that Juliet lived—he would have killed himself if the Nurse and Friar Laurence had not prevented him from so doing. Since the Nurse and Friar Laurence could not always be present in his despairing moments and since the temptations to despair are all too common in life, it was with Romeo only a matter of time.

The stars remain in *Romeo and Juliet,* as well as the chance and bad luck of which they are symbols, but the play also offers a better explanation for the downfall of Romeo. It suggests that "a man's character is his fate," as Heraclitus said—a dictum which sums up one pattern of tragic meaning, one aspect of the tragic poet's vision of order in the universe.

In all his later plays, Shakespeare looked within to character, and not to the stars or to chance or luck, for the causes of individual fates:

> The fault, dear Brutus, is not in our stars,
> But in ourselves, that we are underlings.

We come now to the second question: How is the fate of Romeo and Juliet representative of the fate of all lovers: in what sense does the play have universality?

In looking for the answer to this question, we should first notice how neatly balanced are the feelings of the principals in the play. Taking love as a representative emotional experience, Shakespeare stresses both sides of the experience—the joy and exaltation of the lovers when they are united and their anxiety and unhappiness when they are separated. We see the lovers at both extremes of feeling. The balanced pyramidal form of the play, the five-act structure with the turn at the middle following the rise and fall of the fortunes of the principals, parallels the balance between joy and sorrow which Shakespeare's insight finds in human experience. The artistic structure of the play is an outward show of its inner meaning.

In *Romeo and Juliet* the ending is a dramatic summing up of the whole action: the death of the lovers is symbolical of their lives. Each realizes at the end the extremes of good and evil. In one sense they are united forever, as they wished to be; in another sense they are separated forever in death. Here we see not a happy ending, as in a fairy story, and not an unhappy ending, as in some grim naturalistic tale, in which the worm finally is stilled after wriggling on the hook, but a truly tragic ending, in which joy and sorrow are inevitably joined together—a victory in defeat, a victory of the human spirit accompanied by the inevitable defeat of finite human beings.

Shakespearean tragedy is an artistic vision and revelation of a kind of divine justice which regulates the lives of men and women. Through poetic insight, Shakespeare finds a pattern, an order, in the realm of values; through insight he measures the extremes of feeling, which cannot be measured in any other way. Whoever sees in Shakespearean tragedy only a spectacle of suffering, only an unhappy ending, is seeing only half the story, only one side of life. The artist has done his best to present the whole story and both sides of life. For in the relation between the poles of experience, good and evil, he finds order in the universe. First, he finds that the individual fate of the hero is determined by character, not by chance. Second, he finds that the universality of the hero rests on the fact that, like all of us, the hero is fated to experience the extremes of feeling; and, in accordance with his capacity for feeling, in something like balanced and equal measures, when we follow the rise and fall of the hero's fortunes, we feel ourselves joined to him and to all mankind in the justice of a common fate: this is the secret of the reconciliation to suffering which we find in tragedy.

III

At the time of writing *Romeo and Juliet* and *A Midsummer Night's Dream,* Shakespeare must have been deeply impressed by the thought that the same material—the theme of love, for example, or life itself—may be treated as either tragic or comic. At the beginning of *A Midsummer Night's Dream,* the Athenian lovers, Hermia and Lysander, are in a predicament as serious as the plight of Romeo and Juliet; well may Lysander say, "The course of true love never did run smooth." But the roughness in the course of their love turns out to be the laughable ups and downs of comedy while the roughness in the course of Romeo's love turns into a profoundly tragic change of fortune. The story of Pyramus and Thisbe, the play within a play in *A Midsummer Night's Dream* is, in its main outlines, the same as the story of Romeo and Juliet, yet it becomes in production, as Hippolyta says, "the silliest stuff that ever I heard," while the story of Romeo and Juliet becomes in production a great demonstration that order and justice prevail.

What difference in treatment of the same material—what difference in point of view toward the same material—makes possible the difference between comedy and tragedy?

A Midsummer Night's Dream presents the theme of love on three levels: the level of common sense; the level of nonsense, incongruity, and absurdity; and the level of fantasy. The level of common sense is represented by the love and marriage of Theseus and Hippolyta, who provide the necessary contrast to nonsense. The level of nonsense is represented by the Athenian lovers, Lysander, Demetrius, Helena, and Hermia, and by the workmen, Quince, Snug, Bottom, Flute, Snout, and Starveling, who turn the tragic story of Pyramus and Thisbe into a comic revelation of their own inadequacies. The level of fantasy is represented by the loves of Titania and Oberon, and by the juice of the flower called love-in-idleness, which here serves Shakespeare as an explanation of the influence of chance, caprice, and propinquity on love between the sexes. Since two of these levels, sense and nonsense, are always represented in all comedies, they deserve a few words of comment and definition.

The world of sense is the world of orderly and meaningful patterns, both rational and conventional. Its first law is the law of identity, namely, A is A, which "simply expresses the fact that every term and idea which we use in our reasonings" and practical calculations "must remain what it is." Shakespeare, for example, can make "sense" of the world of human values and find a just order in it only if the law of identity holds true. A is A; and if Romeo is Romeo—that is, if we can be sure that Romeo's character does not change or will not change, then we can understand his fate or even in a general way predict it. Similarly, if for Romeo good is to-be-united-with-Juliet and evil is to-be-separated-from-her—if his values do not change—then we can see in the rise and fall of his fortunes a just balance between good and evil.

The world of nonsense is, in contrast, governed by a law which is the exact opposite of the law of identity. A is not always A; A is sometimes B, or C, or D; and for this reason the world of nonsense is a world of disorder and incongruities. The laughable absurdities and incongruities in *A Midsummer Night's Dream* are for the most part direct consequences of this law of change of identity. Every change of identity leads to incongruities or comic ups and downs. Lysander, for example, is first presented to us as the lover of Hermia; later, touched by the juice of the magic flower, he becomes the lover of Helena; still later through magic he becomes the lover of Hermia again: A becomes B, and then becomes A again. Helena, we are told, was once the object of Demetrius' love; she is first presented to us as an unloved maiden; later through magic she is the object of Lysander's love, later still the object of the love of both Lysander and Demetrius; and finally the object of Demetrius' love only. A becomes B, and then becomes C, and then becomes D, and finally becomes A again. And so on with the Athenian lovers.

In contrast, Theseus and Hippolyta, who represent sense, remain what they are throughout the play.

Bottom, that king of the world of nonsense, undergoes a series of "translations." An ass in the eyes of the audience from the beginning, but a man of parts to his fellows, he later becomes through magic an ass in appearance, later the object of Titania's doting, later still the object of her loathing, and later still Bottom once more. Meanwhile, to complicate the scheme, he wishes to become Pyramus in the play, and also Thisbe, and also Lion. (I'll spare you the working out of his "translations" in ABC's.)

The most effective comedy in *A Midsummer Night's Dream* comes from the subtle use of change of identity in the production of the play within the play, "Pyramus and Thisbe." In the world of sense we accept the convention whereby the actor assumes the identity of the part he plays. In the theater Brian Aherne is Romeo, Katharine Cornell is Juliet. Not so in "Pyramus and Thisbe": Shakespeare reverses the convention and changes order into disorder and incongruity, so that the production excites in us uproarious laughter rather than sympathy and insight. Following the convention of the theater, we would accept Lion and forget the actor, but Lion insists on telling us that he is not Lion but Snug the joiner. Similarly, by every device at his command, Shakespeare makes certain that we cannot see Pyramus, Thisbe, Wall, Moonshine, and Lion because we must see Snug, Bottom, Flute,

Snout, and Starveling. By such devices, based on change of identity, first principle in the world of nonsense and incongruity, what might be seen as tragedy must be seen as comedy.

If tragedy reveals significant patterns in experience, demonstrating that character is fate and that men are united in the justice which apportions equal measures of joy and sorrow to each individual, and if comedy reconciles us through laughter to the disorder, the nonsense, the incongruities and absurdities which we meet everywhere in experience, how does the artist, working with the same material, with love or with life itself, make the choice between comedy and tragedy and determine whether we shall respond to his work of art with laughter or with tragic insight? Shakespeare must have thought of this question in some form while he was writing *Romeo and Juliet* and *A Midsummer Night's Dream;* and possibly his answer is to be found in the reply of Theseus to Hippolyta's verdict on the workers' production of "Pyramus and Thisbe": Hippolyta exclaimed, "This is the silliest stuff that ever I heard." And Theseus replied, "The best in this kind are but shadows, and the worst are no worse, if imagination amend them." If there exists anywhere a wiser comment on drama and the theater, I have not read or heard it.

Undoubtedly Shakespeare must have been thinking, as he wrote the reply of Theseus to Hippolyta, that the same imagination which willingly accepts actors as Romeo, or Hamlet, or Macbeth, or Lear, that accepts the past as the present, the stage as a series of faraway places, and fiction as life itself, could also accept, if it were permitted to do so, his "Pyramus and Thisbe." He knew that his "Pyramus and Thisbe," with the incongruities in the diction removed, and with competent actors losing themselves in their parts (including Lion, Moonshine, and Wall), could be successfully presented as tragedy. For he knew that the chief difference between "silly stuff" and profound art is caused by the artist's power to enlist the spectator's imagination. We can be sure that he knew this because in "Pyramus and Thisbe," as we see it, he has deliberately frustrated, for the sake of laughter, our imagination and prevented us at every point from amending the inherent limitations of drama.

Perhaps he was thinking also of the wider question of what difference in the artist's point of view determines whether we shall focus our attention on the underlying order in experience or on its superficial disorder and incongruities. Can the answer be found in imagination understood as sympathetic insight?

In "Pyramus and Thisbe" we are never permitted to see the story from the point of view of the lovers themselves; we see it only from the outside, as detached and unsympathetic observers. Indeed, we are not permitted to see the lovers at all: we see only the incongruity of the workers presuming to play the parts of a highborn couple. Again, we see the Athenian lovers only from the outside. Hermia, Lysander, Demetrius, and Helena— each is identified for us only as the object of another's affection. They have no inwards for us, and since this is so, how can we possibly tell, from watching them, whether character is fate or whether each suffers and enjoys in equal measures?

Our experience in witnessing *Romeo and Juliet* is altogether different. Soon after the beginning, we follow the action with sympathetic insight from within, from the point of view of the lovers themselves. Inwardness— where character and values may be found and measured by insight—becomes for us the only reality. We live with Romeo and Juliet, seeing the world with their eyes, and as we rise and fall with their fortunes, we are carried finally beyond envy and pity and filled with a sense that all men share a common fate.

IV

Can we say, then, that life is comic if we view it chiefly from the outside, as detached observers whose attention is focused mainly on the disorder and incongruities of the surface? And can we say that life is tragic when we view it from within, from the point of view of an individual—our own point of view or that of someone with whom we identify ourselves by sympathetic insight, as we do with Romeo and Juliet?

Walpole's famous dictum that "the world is a comedy to those that think, a tragedy to those who feel" on first consideration may seem to sum up satisfactorily at this point, for the detached, outer view of man, which permits us to smile at nonsense and incongruity, is at least partially the kind of objectivity which we associate with thought. And sympathetic insight, indispensable in the appreciation of tragedy, obviously involves us in the world of feelings and values. But Walpole's equation of the difference between comedy and tragedy with the difference between thought and feeling does not take into account that, in the first place, laughter is itself an emotion and that, therefore, our response even to "pure" comedy is emotional. Secondly, the emotion of laughter mixes freely with other emotions, and this fact explains the existence of various kinds of comedy.

When the comic poet is amused by someone or something that he dislikes, the result is satire; when he is amused by someone or something that he likes, the result is humor. The spirit of *A Midsummer Night's Dream,* for example, is one of good humor rather than of satire. Shakespeare, we feel, likes human beings even while he laughs at them and is not motivated by a desire to change their ways. Their ways, especially the ways of lovers, are often absurd and nonsensical, but Shakespeare does not view these absurdities as a stern moralist or a cynic might.

A Midsummer Night's Dream is saved from cynicism by the third level of the comedy—the level of fantasy, the imaginative level which softens the sharp distinctions between the world of sense and the world of nonsense. If all the changes of identity on the part of the lovers were attributed to caprice and propinquity, the result would be cynicism, but most of them are attributed to magic in the world of fantasy, and the result is a softer, kindlier humor, which transforms our rational distress at chance and disorder into soothing laughter. There is insight in the background of *A Midsummer Night's Dream,* as in all great comedy. The magic juice of the flower called love-in-idleness seems to tell us that if only we knew the true causes of what seems to be mere chance and caprice in affairs of the heart, then even these apparent absurdities would make sense to us. The fact that it is a creature from fairyland, not a man, who exclaims: "Lord, what fools these mortals be!" takes the poison out of the comment.

Nor can tragedy be satisfactorily explained as the view of a man who is only a man of feeling—if such a man exists. Tragedy can best be explained by its appeal to our rational craving for order, for patterns of meaning; it satisfies this craving at the important point where our reason and our feelings unite. Tragedy offers a vision of order in the universe, which we grasp with sympathetic insight and respond to emotionally as we rise and fall, or fall and rise, with the hero's fortunes. Furthermore, tragedy requires artistic objectivity as well as insight. Sympathetic insight alone might tempt Shakespeare—who as artist enjoys the omnipotence of a creator—to save Romeo from the fate which inevitably flows from his character, but artistic objectivity will not permit him to do so. Even Zeus must bow to necessity.

The spectator also views serious drama with a combination of insight and artistic objectivity, and he applauds the tragic artist who offers both as greater than the writer who is tempted by sympathy to sacrifice objectivity and provide us with a happy ending. We readily recognize such writings as one-sided, as untrue to life, as appeals to our weakness.

Thought and feeling are involved in the creation and appreciation of both comedy and tragedy. In seeing each, we experience an intellectual awareness accompanied by appropriate emotional responses. The main difference is that in tragedy our intelligence is directed toward order in the universe; in comedy, toward disorder and incongruity. Without sympathetic insight, we cannot behold the tragic vision of the fate common to all men. Without detachment, we cannot realize the effect of comedy, which transforms the frustrations of reason into laughter. But there is objectivity as well as insight in the tragic vision, and there is always insight in the background of great comedy. The difference between the point of view of tragedy and that of comedy cannot, therefore, be equated simply with the difference between insight and detachment, but rather is to be found in a subtler proportion whereby insight is stressed in tragedy and detachment is stressed in comedy.

JOHN RUSSELL BROWN

from *Shakespeare and His Comedies*

The commonest form in which Shakespeare presents
the mutual recognition of two lovers is the realization of
each other's beauty. For the young lovers in *A Midsummer Night's Dream,* such realization carries its own
conviction of exclusive truth; Hermia will not "choose
love by another's eyes" (I.i. 140), and when Duke
Theseus orders her to marry Demetrius whom her father
favors, she answers in a single line:

> I would my father look'd but with my eyes.
>
> (I.i.56)

Even if a lover is inconstant he will always demand the
use of his own eyes,[1] and neither the authority of a father
nor the force of general opinion can displace a conviction
based on such experience.[2] Some lovers, like Helena,
may live by such a "truth" even though they recognize
that it is exclusive and irrational:

From *Shakespeare and His Comedies* by John Russell Brown. London:
Methuen and Company Ltd., 1957. Reprinted by permission of the publishers.

[1] Cf. *All's Well That Ends Well,* II.iii.115.
[2] Cf. I.i.227–29.

> Things base and vile, holding no quantity,
> Love can transpose to form and dignity:
> Love looks not with the eyes, but with a mind;
> And therefore is wing'd Cupid painted blind: ...
>
> (I.i.232–35)

In this comedy the irrationality of love's choice provides sport rather than grief. The action takes place in a wood where moonlight and fairy influence suspend our belief in lasting hardship; sometimes a bush may seem to be a bear, but contrariwise even a bear may seem to have no more awful reality than a shadow and may vanish as easily. Moreover the dialogue of the lovers is light and agile so that we are not allowed to dwell upon frustration or suffering. When the sport natural to blind Cupid is heightened by Oberon's enchantment of the lovers' eyes and when events befall preposterously, we find that, even in the telling of the "saddest tale," a "merrier hour was never wasted" (II.i.51–57).

But our laughter is not thoughtless, for, by bringing Bottom and his fellows to the wood to rehearse a play for the Duke's nuptials, Shakespeare has contrived a contrast to the lovers' single-minded pursuit of their own visions of beauty. Once more Shakespeare's comic vision is expressed in contrasts and relationships; Bottom is the sober man by whom we judge the intoxicated. When Lysander's eyes have been touched with the magic herb, he rationalizes his new love for Helena in the loftiest terms:

> Not Hermia but Helena I love:
> Who will not change a raven for a dove?
> The will of man is by his *reason* sway'd;
> And *reason* says you are the worthier maid.
>
> (II.ii.113–16)

Without the agency of magic but simply because Demetrius scorns her, Helena has come to believe that she is as "ugly as a bear" (II.ii.94), and protests, as if it were self-evident:

> ... I did never, no, nor never can,
> Deserve a sweet look from Demetrius' eye.
>
> (II.ii.126–27)

Helena rationally judges that Lysander's love is a "flout" for her own "insufficiency." And when, in the next scene, Titania is charmed to love Bottom whom Puck has disfigured with an ass's head, she too declares her love as if she were convinced by the best of reasons:

> I pray thee, gentle mortal, sing again:
> Mine ear is much enamor'd of thy note;
> So is mine eye enthralled to thy shape;
> And thy fair virtue's force perforce doth move me
> On the first view to say, to swear, I love thee.
>
> (III.i.138–42)

With more modesty in judgment, Bottom answers the other lovers as well as Titania:

> Methinks, mistress, you should have little reason for
> that: and yet, to say the truth, *reason* and love keep little
> company together nowadays; the more the pity that some
> honest neighbors will not make them friends. (III.i.143–47)

Bottom's modesty in judgment is well placed, for life makes fewer demands on him—"if I had wit enough to get out of this wood, I have enough to serve mine own turn" (III.i. 150–52)—he is not asked to love and also to be wise; his judgment is not at the mercy of his eyes.

When Oberon's spell is broken, Bottom seems to have had a strange dream, but it does not count for so much as the helpless game the lovers have played; much as he would like to, Bottom dares not tell his dream, but the lovers must tell theirs, even to the skeptical ear of Theseus. As the vagaries of love and enchantment had seemed perfectly reasonable to those who were involved, and unreasonable or ridiculous to those who had only observed, so the whole action in the wood, once the

first sight of day has passed, will seem more real or more
fantastic.

Such reflections are made explicit at the beginning of
Act V, in the dialogue of Theseus and his bride, Hippolyta. And at this point the play is given a new dimen-
sion; previously we had watched the action as if we were
Olympians laughing at the strutting seriousness of mortals; now we seem to take a step backwards and watch
others watching the action:

> 'Tis strange, my Theseus, that these lovers speak of.

> More strange than *true*: I never may believe
> These antique fables, nor these fairy toys.
> Lovers and madmen have such seething brains,
> Such shaping fantasies, that apprehend
> More than cool reason ever comprehends.

(V.i.1–6)

And not content with likening a lover's truth to that of a
madman, Theseus equates these with the poet's:

> The lunatic, the lover and the poet
> Are of imagination all compact:
> One sees more devils than vast hell can hold,
> That is, the madman: the lover, all as frantic,
> Sees Helen's beauty in a brow of Egypt:
> The poet's eye, in a fine frenzy rolling,
> Doth glance from heaven to earth, from earth to heaven;
> And as imagination bodies forth
> The forms of things unknown, the poet's pen
> Turns them to shapes and gives to airy nothing
> A local habitation and a name. . . .

(V.i.7–17)

For a moment, the image in the glass of the stage is
strangely lightened; has the action we have witnessed the
inconsequence of mere contrivance, or has it the con-

stancy of a poet's[3] imagination? Is it "more strange than true," or is there some "truth" in the lovers' visions of beauty, in the moonlight and enchantments, in Oberon's jealousy and Puck's mistaking? Our judgment hesitates with Hippolyta's:

> . . . all the story of the night told over,
> And all their minds transfigured so together,
> More witnesseth than fancy's images
> And grows to something of great constancy;
> But, howsoever, strange and admirable.

(V.i.23–27)

Possibly we know no more than Demetrius, rubbing his eyes in the daylight:

> . . . I wot not by what power—
> But by some power it is. . . .

(IV.i.167–68)

Our reactions will vary, depending on whether we are stalwart like Bottom, disengaged like Puck, or fanciful like lovers, madmen, and poets. From telling an idle story of magic and love's entangling eyes, Shakespeare has led us to contemplate the relationship between nature and the "art" of lovers and poets; he has led us to recognize the absurdity, privacy, and "truth" of human imagination.[4]

Hard on the heels of this questioning moment, comes talk of a masque or a play to "beguile The lazy time" (V.i.40–41); this, it seems, is "where we came in." But for the "second time round" the perspective will be changed and we shall watch others watching the play.

---

[3] In Shakespeare's day "poet" was used in a general sense after Greek and Latin usage: "One who makes or composes works of literature; an author, writer" (*N.E.D.*, s.v. Ib); it is used for "dramatist" in *Hamlet*, II.ii. See also B. Jonson, "To the memory of my beloved, The Author" prefixed to the Shakespeare 1623 Folio.

[4] The beginning of Act V which gives this new perspective, shows signs of revision; Sir Walter Greg believes that it represents Shakespeare's last touches to his play before handing it over to the book-keeper in the theater (*First Folio* [1955], p. 242).

For us this will be the chief interest of the performance, for, having watched rehearsals, we know precisely the kind of play to expect; again it will be about love and again it will take place by moonlight, but this time the plot will end disastrously. Our interest will lie in whether or not the performance will also be disastrous.

The actors are fully confident; they are so sure of their make-believe that, for fear of frightening the ladies, they must take special precautions before they draw a sword or let their lion roar.[5] But we may doubt whether they will get any help from their text:

> . . . for in all the play
> There is not one word apt, one player fitted.
>
> (V.i.64–65)

As with the pageant at the end of *Love's Labor's Lost,* the actors are at the mercy of their audience, their success depending on the audience's ability to be sufficiently generous, gentle, and humble to "bestow . . . the sense of hearing."[6] We cannot be confident of the outcome. Theseus has previously "pick'd a welcome" from the silence of those who, having prepared entertainment for him, have throttled

> . . . their practiced accent in their fears
> And in conclusion dumbly have broke off,
> Not paying me a welcome.
>
> (V.i.97–99)

but he is also apt to measure lovers' fancies and "antique fables" by the comprehension of "cool reason." As for the young lovers, we know that they are inclined to believe their own dreams, but we have no proof that they will accept in generosity all that "simpleness and duty tender" (V.i.83).

In the event the actors put their faith, as the lovers had done before them, in the "truth" of their fiction:

5 Cf.III.i.9–46.
6 *Love's Labor Lost,* V.ii.669–70.

Gentles, perchance you wonder at this show;
But wonder on, till *truth* make all things plain.

(V.i.127–28)

and again:

This loam, this roughcast and this stone doth show
That I am that same wall; the *truth* is so. . . .

(V.i.161–62)

But the response wavers, and Bottom has to interfere to correct a wrong impression:

The wall, methinks, being sensible, should curse again.

No, in *truth*, sir, he should not. "Deceiving me" is Thisby's cue: she is to enter now, . . . You shall see, it will fall pat as I told you.

(V.i.182–87)

Bottom's faith is invincible, but he cannot ensure success, and Hippolyta judges frankly that the play is "the silliest stuff" that she has ever heard (V.i.211).

At this point Theseus reminds them all of the nature of their entertainment:

The best in this kind are but shadows; and the worst are no worse, if imagination amend them.

It must be your imagination then, and not theirs.

If we imagine no worse of them than they of themselves, they may pass for excellent men.

(V.i.212–17)

In this spirit, Theseus welcomes the entering actors:

Here come two noble beasts in, a man and a lion.

The actors struggle to the end of their play: Moon, unable to complete his prepared speech by reason of the reception he is given, gamely, if somewhat tetchily, substitutes his own less fanciful words; Bottom, with even more fortitude, leaves off talking once, as Pyramus, he

is supposed to be dead, and he waits until the play is
done before he rises to correct his audience and offer
an epilogue.

So, unlike the pageant of the Worthies, the "tedious
brief scene" of Pyramus and Thisbe is completed. Theseus
refuses the epilogue:

> No epilogue, I pray you; for your play needs no ex-
> cuse. Never excuse; for when the players are all dead,
> there need none to be blamed.   (V.i.357–59)

"Truly" it has been a "fine tragedy" (V.i.362) and
the players can celebrate with a Bergomask, a joyful
country dance which is natural to their elation and
abilities. Then Theseus must recall the lovers from the
fiction they have been watching:

> The iron tongue of midnight hath told twelve:
> Lovers, to bed; 'tis almost fairy time.
>   (V.i.365–66)

The "palpable-gross play" has beguiled the time, and
they must now to their own parts. And as they file off
in due order for the next scene, the fairies enter from
the enchanted wood and, following them, bring blessing
on their action.

If one wished to describe the judgment which informs
A Midsummer Night's Dream, one might do so very
simply: the play suggests that lovers, like lunatics, poets,
and actors, have their own "truth" which is established
as they see the beauty of their beloved, and that they are
confident in this truth for, although it seems the "silliest
stuff" to an outsider, to them it is quite reasonable; it
also suggests that lovers, like actors, need, and sometimes
ask for, our belief, and that this belief can only be
given if we have the generosity and imagination to think
"no worse of them than they of themselves."

The play's greatest triumph is the manner in which our

wavering acceptance of the illusion of drama is used as a kind of flesh-and-blood image of the acceptance which is appropriate to the strange and private "truth" of those who enact the play of love. By using this living image, Shakespeare has gone beyond direct statement in words or action and has presented his judgment in terms of a mode of being, a relationship, in which we, the audience, are actually involved. And he has ensured that this image is experienced at first hand, for the audience of the play-within-the-play does not make the perfect reaction; one of them describes what this entails but it is left for us to make that description good. The success of the play will, finally, depend upon our reaction to its shadows.[7]

[7] So Puck assures us; cf.V.i.425–40.

Suggested References

The number of possible references is vast and grows alarmingly. (The *Shakespeare Quarterly* devotes a substantial part of one issue each year to a list of the previous year's work, and *Shakespeare Survey*—an annual publication—includes a substantial review of recent scholarship, as well as an occasional essay surveying a few decades of scholarship on a chosen topic.) Though no works are indispensable, those listed below have been found helpful.

1. Shakespeare's Times

Byrne, M. St. Clare. *Elizabethan Life in Town and Country.* Rev. ed. New York: Barnes & Noble, Inc., 1961. Chapters on manners, beliefs, education, etc., with illustrations.

Craig, Hardin. *The Enchanted Glass: the Elizabethan Mind in Literature.* New York and London: Oxford University Press, 1936. The Elizabethan intellectual climate.

Nicoll, Allardyce (ed.). *The Elizabethans.* London: Cambridge University Press, 1957. An anthology of Elizabethan writings, especially valuable for its illustrations from paintings, title pages, etc.

Shakespeare's England. 2 vols. Oxford: The Clarendon Press, 1916. A large collection of scholarly essays on a wide variety of topics (e.g., astrology, costume, gardening, horsemanship), with special attention to Shakespeare's references to these topics.

Tillyard, E. M. W. *The Elizabethan World Picture*. London: Chatto & Windus, 1943; New York: The Macmillan Company, 1944. A brief account of some Elizabethan ideas of the universe.

Wilson, John Dover (ed.). *Life in Shakespeare's England*. 2nd ed. New York: The Macmillan Company, 1913. An anthology of Elizabethan writings on the countryside, superstition, education, the court, etc.

2. Shakespeare

Bentley, Gerald E. *Shakespeare: A Biographical Handbook*. New Haven, Conn.: Yale University Press, 1961. The facts about Shakespeare, with virtually no conjecture intermingled.

Bradby, Anne (ed.). *Shakespeare Criticism, 1919–1935*. London: Oxford University Press, 1936. A small anthology of excellent essays on the plays.

Bush, Geoffrey Douglas. *Shakespeare and the Natural Condition*. Cambridge, Mass.: Harvard University Press; London: Oxford University Press, 1956. A short, sensitive account of Shakespeare's view of "Nature," touching most of the works.

Chute, Marchette. *Shakespeare of London*. New York: E. P. Dutton & Co., Inc., 1949. A readable biography fused with portraits of Stratford and London life.

Clemen, Wolfgang H. *The Development of Shakespeare's Imagery*. Cambridge, Mass.: Harvard University Press, 1951. (Originally published in German, 1936.) A temperate account of a subject often abused.

Chambers, E. K. *William Shakespeare: A Study of Facts and Problems*. 2 vols. London: Oxford University Press, 1930. An invaluable, detailed reference work; not for the casual reader.

Craig, Hardin. *An Interpretation of Shakespeare*. New York: Citadel Press, 1948. A scholar's book designed for the layman. Comments on all the works.

Dean, Leonard F. (ed.). *Shakespeare: Modern Essays in Criticism*. New York: Oxford University Press, 1957. Mostly mid-twentieth-century critical studies, covering Shakespeare's artistry.

Granville-Barker, Harley. *Prefaces to Shakespeare*. 2 vols. Princeton, N.J.: Princeton University Press, 1946–47. Essays on ten plays by a scholarly man of the theater.

Harbage, Alfred. *As They Liked It*. New York: The Macmillan Company, 1947. A sensitive, long essay on Shakespeare, morality, and the audience's expectations.

Smith, D. Nichol (ed.). *Shakespeare Criticism*. New York: Oxford University Press, 1916. A selection of criticism from 1623 to 1840, ranging from Ben Jonson to Thomas Carlyle.

Spencer, Theodore. *Shakespeare and the Nature of Man*. New York: The Macmillan Company, 1942. Shakespeare's plays in relation to Elizabethan thought.

Stoll, Elmer Edgar. *Shakespeare and Other Masters*. Cambridge, Mass.: Harvard University Press; London: Oxford University Press, 1940. Essays on tragedy, comedy, and aspects of dramaturgy, with special reference to some of Shakespeare's plays.

Traversi, D. A. *An Approach to Shakespeare*. Rev. ed. New York: Doubleday & Co., Inc., 1956. An analysis of the plays, beginning with words, images, and themes, rather than with characters.

Van Doren, Mark. *Shakespeare*. New York: Henry Holt & Company, Inc., 1939. Brief, perceptive readings of all of the plays.

Whitaker, Virgil K. *Shakespeare's Use of Learning*. San Marino, Calif.: Huntington Library, 1953. A study of the relation of Shakespeare's reading to his development as a dramatist.

3. Shakespeare's Theater

Adams, John Cranford. *The Globe Playhouse*. Rev. ed.

New York: Barnes & Noble, Inc., 1961. A detailed conjecture about the physical characteristics of the theater Shakespeare often wrote for.

Beckerman, Bernard. *Shakespeare at the Globe, 1599–1609*. New York: The Macmillan Company, 1962. On the playhouse and on Elizabethan dramaturgy, acting, and staging.

Chambers, E. K. *The Elizabethan Stage*. 4 vols. New York: Oxford University Press, 1923. Reprinted with corrections, 1945. An indispensable reference work on theaters, theatrical companies, and staging at court.

Harbage, Alfred. *Shakespeare's Audience*. New York: Columbia University Press; London: Oxford University Press, 1941. A study of the size and nature of the theatrical public.

Hodges, C. Walter. *The Globe Restored*. London: Ernest Benn, Ltd., 1953; New York: Coward-McCann, Inc., 1954. A well-illustrated and readable attempt to reconstruct the Globe Theatre.

Nagler, A. M. *Shakespeare's Stage*. Tr. by Ralph Manheim. New Haven, Conn.: Yale University Press, 1958. An excellent brief introduction to the physical aspect of the playhouse.

Smith, Irwin. *Shakespeare's Globe Playhouse*. New York: Charles Scribner's Sons, 1957. Chiefly indebted to J. C. Adams' controversial book, with additional material and scale drawings for model-builders.

Venezky, Alice S. *Pageantry on the Shakespearean Stage*. New York: Twayne Publishers, Inc., 1951. An examination of spectacle in Elizabethan drama.

4. Miscellaneous Reference Works

Abbott, E. A. *A Shakespearean Grammar*. New edition. New York: The Macmillan Company, 1877. An examination of differences between Elizabethan and modern grammar.

Bartlett, John. *A New and Complete Concordance . . . to*

. . . *Shakespeare*. New York: The Macmillan Company, 1894. An index to most of Shakespeare's words.

Bullough, Geoffrey. *Narrative and Dramatic Sources of Shakespeare*. 4 vols. Vols. 5 and 6 in preparation. New York: Columbia University Press; London: Routledge & Kegan Paul, Ltd., 1957–. A collection of many of the books Shakespeare drew upon.

Greg, W. W. *The Shakespeare First Folio*. New York and London: Oxford University Press, 1955. A detailed yet readable history of the first collection (1623) of Shakespeare's plays.

Kökeritz, Helge. *Shakespeare's Names*. New Haven, Conn.: Yale University Press, 1959; London: Oxford University Press, 1960. A guide to the pronunciation of some 1,800 names appearing in Shakespeare.
———. *Shakespeare's Pronunciation*. New Haven, Conn.: Yale University Press; London: Oxford University Press, 1953. Contains much information about puns and rhymes.

Linthicum, Marie C. *Costume in the Drama of Shakespeare and His Contemporaries*. New York and London: Oxford University Press, 1936. On the fabrics and dress of the age, and references to them in the plays.

Muir, Kenneth. *Shakespeare's Sources*. London: Methuen & Co., Ltd., 1957. Vol. 2 in preparation. The first volume, on the comedies and tragedies, attempts to ascertain what books were Shakespeare's sources, and what use he made of them.

Onions, C. T. *A Shakespeare Glossary*. London: Oxford University Press, 1911; 2nd ed., rev., with enlarged addenda, 1953. Definitions of words (or senses of words) now obsolete.

Partridge, Eric. *Shakespeare's Bawdy*. Rev. ed. New York: E. P. Dutton & Co., Inc.; London: Routledge & Kegan Paul, Ltd., 1955. A glossary of bawdy words and phrases.

Shakespeare Quarterly. See headnote to Suggested References.

Shakespeare Survey. See headnote to Suggested References.

5. *A Midsummer Night's Dream*

Barber, Cesar Lombardi. *Shakespeare's Festive Comedy.* Princeton, N.J.: Princeton University Press; London: Oxford University Press, 1959.

Bonnard, Georges A. "Shakespeare's Purpose in *Midsummer-Night's Dream,*" *Shakespeare Jahrbuch,* XCII (1956), 268–79.

Briggs, K. M. *The Anatomy of Puck.* London: Routledge & Kegan Paul, Ltd., 1959.

Evans, Bertrand. *Shakespeare's Comedies.* New York and London: Oxford University Press, 1960.

Hunter, G. K. *Shakespeare: The Late Comedies.* London: Longmans, Green & Co., Ltd., 1962.

Kermode, Frank. "The Mature Comedies," *Stratford-upon-Avon Studies III: The Early Shakespeare,* ed. John Russell Brown and Bernard Harris. London: Edward Arnold (Publishers) Ltd., 1961; New York: St Martin's Press, Inc., 1962.

Nemerov, Howard. "The Marriage of Theseus and Hippolyta," *Kenyon Review,* XVIII (1956), 633–41.

Olsen, Paul A. "*A Midsummer-Night's Dream* and the Meaning of Court Marriage," *ELH; A Journal of English Literary History,* XXIV (1957), 95–119.

Schanzer, Ernest. "The Moon and the Fairies in *A Midsummer-Night's Dream,*" *University of Toronto Quarterly,* XXIV (1955), 234–46.

Siegel, Paul N. "*A Midsummer-Night's Dream* and the Wedding Guests," *Shakespeare Quarterly,* IV (1953), 139–44.

Watkins, Ronald. *Moonlight at the Globe: An Essay in Shakespeare Production Based on Performance of "A Midsummer-Night's Dream" at Harrow School.* London: Michael Joseph, Ltd., 1946.

THE COMPLETE PLAYS OF SHAKESPEARE

Superlatively edited paperbound volumes of Shakespeare's complete plays. Under the general editorship of Sylvan Barnet, Chairman of the English Department of Tufts University, each volume features a general Introduction by Dr. Barnet; special Introduction and Notes by an eminent Shakespearean scholar, critical commentary from past and contemporary authorities, and when possible, the actual source of the play. Its entirety or in excerpt. The volumes already published, priced at only 50¢ each, include:

Plays in MENTOR and SIGNET Books

THE GENIUS OF THE EARLY ENGLISH THEATER
Barnet, Berman and Burto, editors

Complete plays including three anonymous plays—"Abraham and Isaac," "The Second Shepherd's Play," and "Everyman," and Marlowe's "Doctor Faustus," Shakespeare's "Macbeth," Jonson's "Volpone," and Milton's "Samson Agonistes." Also includes critical essays.

(#MQ438—95¢)

THE GENIUS OF THE LATER ENGLISH THEATER
Barnet, Berman and Burto, editors

Complete plays, including Congreve's "The Way of the World," Goldsmith's "She Stoops to Conquer," Byron's "Manfred," Wilde's "Importance of Being Earnest," Shaw's "Major Barbara," and Golding's "The Brass Butterfly." With critical essays. (#MQ448—95¢)

THE GENIUS OF THE IRISH THEATER
Barnet, Berman and Burto, editors

Complete texts of seven plays by Shaw, Synge, Lady Gregory, William Butler Yeats, Jack B. Yeats, Frank O'Connor, and Sean O'Casey. With critical essays. (#MT315—75¢)

PLAYS *by George Bernard Shaw*

"Arms and the Man," "Candida," "Man and Superman," and "Mrs. Warren's Profession." Introduction by Eric Bentley. (#CT301—75¢)

EIGHT GREAT COMEDIES *Barnet, Berman and Burto, editors*

Complete English texts of "The Clouds," Machiavelli's "Mandragola," "Twelfth Night," "The Miser," "The Beggar's Opera," "Importance of Being Earnest," "Uncle Vanya," "Arms and the Man." With essays on the comic view. (#MQ461—95¢)

EIGHT GREAT TRAGEDIES *Barnet, Berman and Burto, editors*

Complete English texts of "Prometheus Bound," "Oedipus the King," "Hippolytus," "King Lear," "Ghosts," "Miss Julie," "On Baile's Strand," and "Desire Under the Elms." With essays on the tragic view. (#MQ343—95¢)

THE GENIUS OF THE FRENCH THEATER *Albert Bermel, editor*

Complete texts in English of plays by Moliere, Racine, Beaumarchais, Hugo, Rostand, Labiche, Giraudoux and Anouilh. With essays on the French theater.

(#MQ366—95¢)

SIGNET CLASSICS
from Around the World

QUENTIN DURWARD *by Sir Walter Scott*

A romantic story of adventure in fifteenth-century France. Afterword by Denis W. Brogan. (#CT181—75¢)

IDYLLS OF THE KING and a Selection of Poems
by Alfred Lord Tennyson

The famous Arthurian romance and other poetry by the Victorian Poet Laureate. Foreword by George Barker.
(#CT286—75¢)

THE TRAVELS OF MARCO POLO

The enduring record of Marco Polo's thirty-five years of fabulous Eastern travel. Edited with an Introduction by Milton Rugoff. (#CD97—50¢)

CANDIDE, ZADIG and Selected Stories *by Voltaire*

Voltaire satirizes with ruthless wit the social, religious, and human vanities of his day in sixteen biting stories. A new translation with an Introduction by Donald Frame.
(#CD35—50¢)

RESURRECTION *by Leo Tolstoy*

The Russian master's final work tells the story of a young man who seeks salvation by following into exile the girl for whose career in crime he was responsible. Translated by Vera Traill with a Foreword by Alan Hodge.
(#CT63—75¢)

OLIVER TWIST *by Charles Dickens*

Dickens' classic indictment of the orphanages and crime-ridden slums of 19th Century London. Afterword by Edward La Comte. (#CP102—60¢)

THE SCARLET LETTER *by Nathaniel Hawthorne*

A masterpiece by one of America's fine 19th Century writers, this is the story of a proud and sinful woman in Puritan New England. Foreword by Leo Marx. (#CD8—50¢)

ROBINSON CRUSOE *by Daniel Defoe*

The timeless story of a young merchant seaman's struggle for survival when he is marooned on an uninhabited island. Afterword by Harvey Swados.   (#CD55—50¢)

THE MARRIAGES and Other Stories *by Henry James*

Nine rarely anthologized stories by the master of sophisticated irony. Foreword by Eleanor M. Tilton.

(#CD87—50¢)

MAIN STREET *by Sinclair Lewis*

The crusade of a doctor's wife against the narrow-minded conventions of a small town. Afterword by Mark Schorer.

(#CQ352—95¢)

BABBITT *by Sinclair Lewis*

The caustic portrayal of an American go-getter, ready and willing to sacrifice his principles to get ahead. Afterword by Mark Schorer.   (#CQ344—95¢)

THE MUTINY ON BOARD H.M.S. BOUNTY *by William Bligh*

The captain's own account of the most famous mutiny to take place in the South Seas. Afterword by Milton Rugoff.

(#CP94—60¢)

BILLY BUDD and Other Tales *by Herman Melville*

The title story and other outstanding short stories, including the *Piazza Tales*, by the author of *Moby Dick*. Afterword by Williard Thorp.   (#CT75—75¢)

ADVENTURES IN THE SKIN TRADE and Other Stories
     by Dylan Thomas

Brilliant and fantastic tales by the great Welsh poet, who writes of sinners and lovers, nature and madness. Afterword by Vernon Watkins.   (#CT341—75¢)